My World of THE PAST

Ralph Whitlock

HAMLYN
London · New York · Sydney · Toronto

Published 1975 by
THE HAMLYN PUBLISHING GROUP LIMITED
London · New York · Sydney · Toronto
Astronaut House, Hounslow Road, Feltham, Middlesex,
England

ISBN 0 600 36188 8

Printed by Litografía A. Romero, S. A.
Tenerife (Spain). D. L. TF. 481 - 1975

Contents

Ancient Egypt

This book is about empires and cities and the great civilizations of the past. It is about how people lived and the wonderful things they did. First, however, we must ask ourselves why people should want to live together in cities and form civilizations.

Early men were hunters. They followed flocks and herds of wild animals and killed what they needed for food, much as lions do in Africa today. They did not even have permanent villages. But men ate berries, fruits and seeds besides meat, and, after a time, they discovered that if they planted seeds in good soil they could grow much more food than they could gather by searching for it. So they settled down in places where there was good soil and water. They put fences around the good soil, to keep out wild animals and strange men. They tamed some of the wild animals, such as sheep, goats and cows, so that they would have a supply of meat and milk.

In the beginning each man, or family, did everything for himself. When men started farming and settled in permanent villages, however, it became possible for men to become experts at certain trades. A smith would spend all his time working metal. He would not bother to grow food or hunt for it. He would exchange his metal-work for other goods that he needed. In the same way, weavers, potters and other craftsmen worked at their own trades. There were also soldiers who protected the village, musicians who sang songs and entertained the people, and, later, when the villages had grown into towns, scribes who wrote letters and kept accounts (after people had learned how to write) and many others with special skills.

Left: Early Men lived by hunting. They made shelters from animal skins, and tools from rocks and bones. These people were the first artists.

Far Left: The oldest piece of cloth in existence dates from 6500 B.C. This Berber woman is using the same method of spinning.

Below: A selection of weapons and tools made from flint, wood and bone. Fishing was done by means of hooks, harpoons, nets and traps.

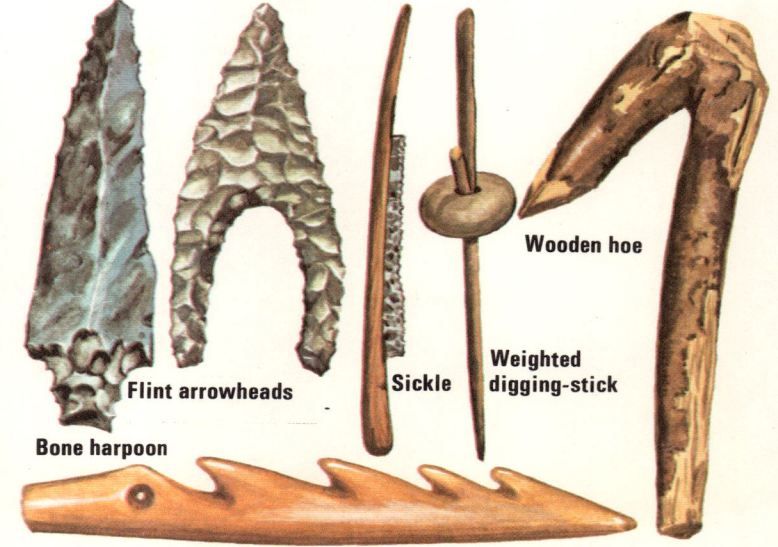

Flint arrowheads

Bone harpoon

Sickle

Wooden hoe

Weighted digging-stick

All these tradesmen and craftsmen did not need fields of their own, so they lived quite close together. It was good to be able to do this, because they could then build a wall around the settlement, to keep out their enemies. Inside the wall they lived, clustered together, in streets. In the centre of the enclosure there was an open space, or square, where they used to meet to exchange their goods for food or whatever else they needed, and also to talk with each other. This was the way the first cities grew when men came to live together for trade and defence against their enemies.

Later, many cities combined together to form a kingdom or an empire. Or, more often, they were conquered by some great soldier who had formed a powerful army. In the following pages we shall read about some of the greatest empires. It is worth remembering that they were all composed of hundreds of cities, towns and villages which grew up in the way described.

The first need, then, for the change from hunting to a settled life in villages was good soil. There also had to be a good climate, which would help crops to grow well. And there had to be plenty of water. All early civilizations started in places which met these needs.

Scale of Metres

0 50 100 200 300 400

Above: Plan of the city of Ur, showing the main buildings from all periods. Ur is one of the oldest cities that have been excavated in the world.

Left: Wild cattle, pigs and goats were reared for meat and milk. Their skins were used for clothing and their bones were used for tools and weapons. Leather was also used for bowls and water-carriers.

7

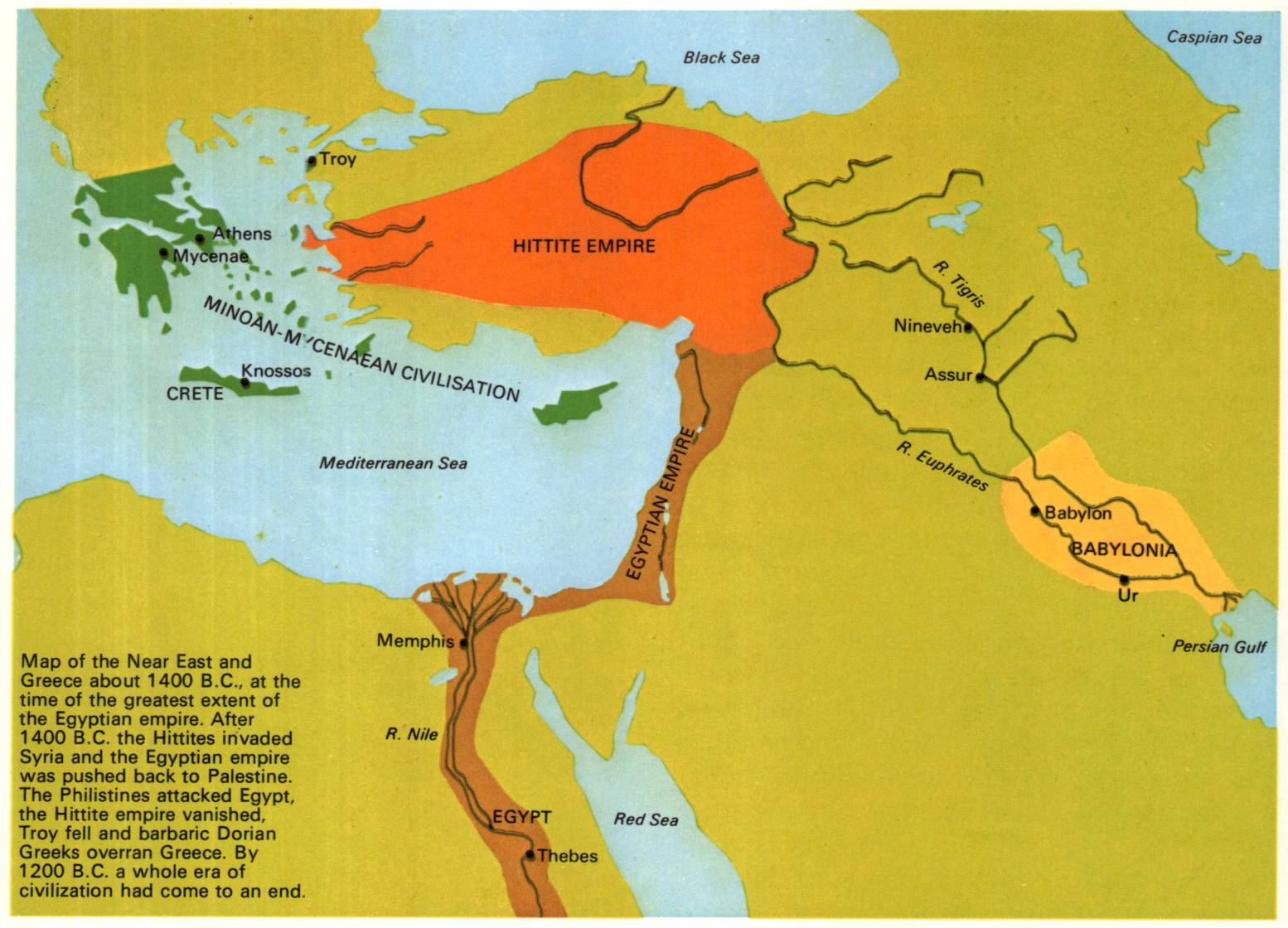

Map of the Near East and Greece about 1400 B.C., at the time of the greatest extent of the Egyptian empire. After 1400 B.C. the Hittites invaded Syria and the Egyptian empire was pushed back to Palestine. The Philistines attacked Egypt, the Hittite empire vanished, Troy fell and barbaric Dorian Greeks overran Greece. By 1200 B.C. a whole era of civilization had come to an end.

One of the earliest civilizations of all began in Egypt. Egypt is in the north-east corner of Africa. If we look at the map we shall see that one of the longest rivers in the world, the Nile, runs through it from south to north, and that the country is surrounded by desert.

Egypt is a warm country because it is near the tropics. Snow never falls, and the river Nile provides plenty of fresh water. It also provides another treasure. Every August, the level of the river rises. A great flood of water, carrying masses of mud, pours down into Egypt from the mountains at the source of the river Nile. Flooding occurs far beyond the usual banks of the river and spreads over all the fields. When the water drains away, the fields are left covered with a layer of mud which is extremely fertile. Egyptian farmers hurry to plant their seeds in this new soil. The seeds quickly grow under the hot sun, and soon the farmers are able to reap a

harvest which is stored for the winter.

Life in Egypt depends on the annual flooding of the Nile. Early Egyptian writers said, rightly, that Egypt was the gift of the Nile. The Egyptians did not know where the floods came from. We know now. The Nile rises in the great mountains and lakes of central Africa. Every summer heavy rains fall on the mountains, and the water drains into the Nile. So the mud which provides Egyptian farmers with the fertile soil they need is washed from the mountains of Ethiopia.

Although the Nile floods usually arrived at the proper time, occasionally they did not. If they failed, there was famine. If they rose too high, there was much damage and loss of life. So from very early times the Egyptians anxiously watched the river when the floods were due. They devised an instrument called a Nilometer, for measuring the rate at which the water level rose.

They also learned to control the floods, in order to make the best use of the water and mud. Most of Egypt consists of a narrow strip of fertile land on either side of the river. Beyond lies the desert. But the river divides about 100 kilometres from the sea. It splits into two main streams and hundreds of smaller ones. These flow through a vast, green, flat plain called the Nile delta. It is criss-crossed with ditches and drainage channels to bring the life-giving water and mud to every field. Most Egyptians have always lived here.

If it were not for the Nile floods, Egypt would be a desert country. On the very rare occasions when rain does fall it causes a great deal of damage. If there is heavy rainfall, houses are destroyed. They just collapse and ooze away because they are made of mud.

Egyptian houses have flat roofs, and it is pleasant to sit out on them and look across the fields and palm trees in the cool of the evening. There is, of course, no need for sloping roofs to drain off the rain, and the houses have few windows. The sunlight is so bright, it is pleasant to step inside a house that is dark and cool. Most houses are built around a courtyard, with the windows and doors opening into it.

Egyptian villagers were building houses like these and growing their crops in the Nile mud thousands of years ago. In time some of the villages grew into cities, and the cities were linked together to become a kingdom. The king of Egypt was called a Pharaoh. The first Pharaoh successfully united Egypt into one kingdom in about the year 3200 B.C.—more than five thousand years ago.

Left: Egypt is criss-crossed with irrigation ditches bringing water from the Nile.

Below Left: This picture shows the grapes being trodden after the grape harvest.

Below: Corn being winnowed to separate the grain from the chaff. Winnowing was done by hand, and often at night because there was more wind.

9

With millions of people working in the fields, making things and engaging in trade, Egypt became a very rich country. Mud houses were good enough for ordinary people, but the Pharaoh and his dignitaries wanted something better. Although the land near the river Nile was of fertile soil and mud, the hills of the desert on either side contained stone which could be quarried. So the Pharaohs started to build palaces, temples and tombs of stone.

Often, people built pillars in front of their houses, partly for ornament and partly to help support the roof and to act as door-posts. These pillars were made of bundles of reeds, cut from the river banks and tied together. So when the builders using stone wanted to make pillars they carved them to look like bundles of reeds. We can see many of these stone pillars today. They have long parallel lines carved down them, to look like reed stems, and are decorated at the top to look like the reed flower-heads.

These people believed in a life after death, and they believed that they must take everything that they needed in this life, including the body, into their life after death. So they put everything they might need, such as food, furniture, clothes, jewellery and even toys for children in their tombs. As they wanted their bodies to be preserved, they perfected an art known as embalming. The parts of a dead body most likely to decay were taken away and replaced by spices. Then the body was tightly bound in strips of cloth and sealed in a kind of coffin. A body treated in this way was called a mummy. Many Egyptian mummies have been found, enabling us to see what Egyptians looked like so long ago.

The Pharaohs knew that there were many robbers in the world. They knew that a time might come when thieves would try to break into the tombs, in order to steal the treasures stored there. So some of the early Pharaohs had the idea of hiding the room in which their mummies and all their treasures were buried in the heart of a huge stone building. This is what the pyramids were used for, and they are still visited by thousands of people every year who come to Egypt to see them. The rooms which contain the graves of kings are very carefully hidden inside.

Above: The sarcophagus of Tutankhamun, 1362–1263 B.C.

Right: A wooden figure of an Egyptian girl playing a harp, about 850 B.C.

Left: A guest-hall made from reeds in a marsh village in southern Mesopotamia.

One of the pyramids, the Step Pyramid, built about 2770 B.C., is supposed to be the oldest stone building in the world. The Great Pyramid is still one of the largest buildings in the world. It rests on a square base, and its sides are 226.8 metres long. Its height is 135 metres. It is made of 2,300,000 stone blocks each one weighing more than $2\frac{1}{2}$ tonnes. The pyramids were covered with a facing of white limestone. Now it has been worn away and a series of steps is all that remains.

When the pyramids were built, the Egyptians had not discovered the use of pulleys, winches or cranes. So each stone block had to be taken from the quarries and hauled up the sides of the pyramid by man-power. It is supposed that the blocks were moved on wooden rollers. More than 100,000 men were needed to build one pyramid.

Not far from the Great Pyramid there stands another huge stone figure, the Sphinx. It is carved from a limestone hill and represents the figure of a lion with a man's head. A temple stood between its front paws.

Above: 1. The four sons of Horus, about 1000 B.C.
2. Fish vase made of pottery about 1365 B.C. **3.** A glass vase and jug about 1475 B.C.

Right: The Great Pyramid and the Sphinx.

The Egyptians invented the art of writing quite early in their history. At first they used only picture signs, but later they developed a kind of alphabet. Egyptian writing is full of picture signs, such as those of hawks, lions, bill-hooks, owls, eyes, jackals, shepherd's crooks and other everyday things. In our alphabet we have 26 signs, or letters. The Egyptians had to learn 700 signs. Their system of writing is known as *hieroglyphics.*

The walls of tombs and other buildings in Egypt are covered with hieroglyphics. For a long time, no-one could read them. Then, in 1799, a stone was dug up in Egypt, near Rosetta, bearing the same inscription in two languages. One was ancient Greek, which was known. The other was ancient Egyptian, in two types of writing. So, by putting the two together, scholars were able to understand how Egyptian hieroglyphics should be read. This famous stone is known as the Rosetta stone.

Besides carving inscriptions on walls, the Egyptians invented a new kind of material for writing on, made from a reed called papyrus. It is from this word that we get our word 'paper'. Papyrus was very like the paper we use today.

Because of the very dry climate, things do not decay nearly as quickly as they do in rainier lands. Papyrus can lie buried in the desert sand for centuries without rotting. Therefore, enormous numbers of Egyptian documents have survived for us to read— history books, account books, letters from schoolboys to their parents, lesson books, love letters, books of psalms and prayers, law books and text books.

For hundreds of years the Egyptians were content to stay in their own country. With their river providing everything they needed, they were not very interested in things outside Egypt. Then, one day, in about the year 1720 B.C., the country was invaded by a vast horde of people from the east. They destroyed many of the cities, killed people and made many more slaves. Their leader became the Pharaoh, and for more than 150 years his descendants ruled Egypt. They were known as the Hyksos, or Shepherd, Kings.

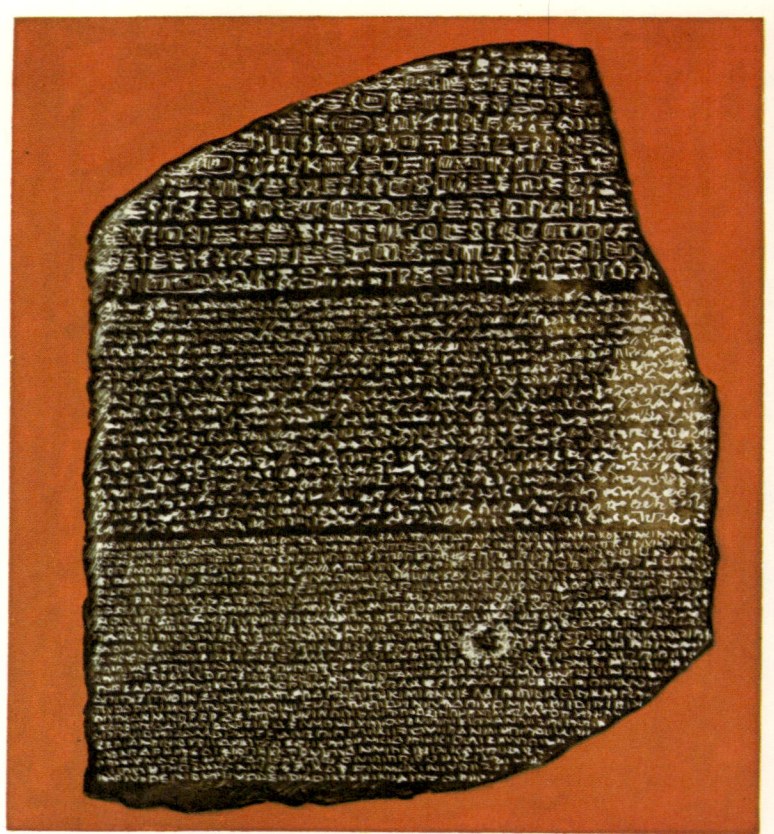

Above: The Rosetta stone was dug up by a French officer in 1799. Its parallel inscriptions in three different scripts provided the key to understanding ancient Egyptian writing.

Then they were driven out by the Egyptians. The new kings had learned a lesson. They knew they must take an interest in the world outside Egypt. So Egyptian armies marched through Palestine and conquered all the country as far north as the river Euphrates. Ships sailed on the Mediterranean sea, bringing cedar wood from the mountains of Lebanon and trading with the island of Crete. Other ships sailed on the Red Sea, going as far as a mysterious land called Punt, from which they brought back gold, spices and strange animals.

Egyptian armies also marched up the Nile for many hundreds of kilometres, into the land of Nubia. And in the desert of Sinai, slaves working for the Egyptians mined turquoise and other precious stones.

European countries reckon their early history by families of kings, called dynasties. In England there were, for instance, the Plantagenet and Tudor dynasties; in France, the Valois and Bourbon dynasties. Egypt, which has a far longer history than any European country, had thirty dynasties.

The last native Egyptian dynasty came to an end when Alexander the Great conquered Egypt in 322 B.C. Thereafter, it was ruled by Greek kings until just before the time of Christ, when the Romans took over. Under the Greeks and Romans, Egypt was one of the richest countries in the world. Its greatest city, Alexandria, which had been founded by Alexander the Great, was very like some of the best of our modern cities. The country produced vast quantities of grain each year, much of which was sent to feed the people of Rome.

Egypt continued in the Roman Empire until the year A.D. 638, when it was conquered by the Arabs. Under Arab rule it again became a rich and important country. Cairo, which was founded by the Arabs, became, and still is, the largest Arab city in the world. For most of the ordinary people of Egypt, however, life is still much the same as it was in the far-off days of the Pharaohs.

Left: This tomb, with its hieroglyphics, shows the vivid way in which the Egyptians expressed their belief in the afterworld. Anubis is preparing to lead the dead man to the judgement seat.

Above: Thoth, the god of writing, mathematics, the seasons, in fact everything requiring exactness.

13

The Fertile Crescent

We have seen in the previous chapter how the people of ancient Egypt lived in a land almost cut off from the rest of the world. Deserts surrounded their country on almost every side. A few bolder Egyptians who tried to travel up the Nile, to see where the floods came from, found their way blocked by great waterfalls, called cataracts, and by a vast marsh. Only at the north-east corner of Egypt was there a link with other fertile lands. Egyptians could walk along the sea-shore to the beginning of another fertile land, the country of Palestine.

If we look at a map we see that Palestine was a narrow ribbon of land stretching south to north along the eastern shore of the Mediterranean sea. It is a hilly country, bounded on the east by the very deep valley of the river Jordan. Crossing the river Jordan, we soon find ourselves in desert again.

If we continue northwards, we come to mountains, the mountains of Lebanon, which in ancient times were covered with mighty cedar trees. Beyond is the land of Syria; its northern boundary is the river Euphrates.

Here we turn right and follow the river down to its mouth. It flows into the warm sea known as the Persian Gulf, more than 1000 kilometres away. Not very far away, to the north-east, another great river, the Tigris, flows in the same direction. Both these rivers flow into the Persian Gulf.

If we look again at the way we have travelled we see we have moved in a vast semi-circle, or crescent. When we started we were facing north-east; now we are facing south-east. All the time we have been travelling in fertile country, with trees, grass and rivers. But on our right the desert has never been far away. On our left, lay first the sea and then ranges of mountains. We can understand why this crescent-shaped strip of land became known as *The Fertile Crescent.*

Above: This map shows the area covered by the Fertile Crescent.

Right: A silver rein ring found in Ur, dating from 2500 B.C.

Right: A Sumerian war chariot.

Right: A Sumerian figure in terra-cotta.

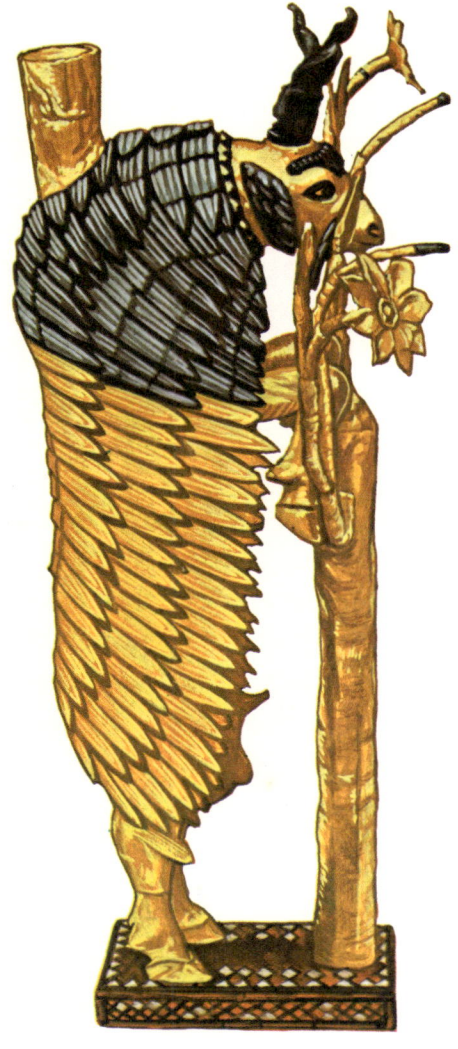

Above: A goat with its front feet on the branches of a tree. This was found in the 'Great Death Pit' in Ur.

Below: A clay tablet inscribed in cuneiform script, and a copper bison made about 2500 B.C.

The Euphrates and Tigris are in some ways like the river Nile. Each spring they bring down mud in floodwater, as the snows on the northern mountains melt. In very early times, men found fertile soil here, a pleasant climate and a wealth of wild animals, birds, fish and plants. So they settled in the area and built villages and then cities, just as the Egyptians did. The first cities were founded there at least nine thousand years ago.

One of the first civilized people about whom we know anything were the Sumerians. The names of some of their cities are mentioned in the Book of Genesis, in the Bible. Ur, the birthplace of Abraham, is the most famous. The Sumerians did not form a great empire until late in their history. By 3000 B.C. each city had its own government, and these cities often made war against each other.

The Sumerians were very intelligent people. They learned how to control the floodwaters of the rivers by means of a network of irrigation ditches. These ditches extended right into the desert. They made bricks from mud dried in the sun. They learned how to make bronze by mixing tin and copper, and they were skilled at making bronze tools and weapons.

Two important inventions, however, stand out from the rest. The Sumerians learned how to make and use wheels, and they also invented a form of writing.

Their writing developed more quickly than that of the Egyptians. Egyptian hieroglyphics were a form of picture writing in which many of the symbols were pictures, but the Sumerians developed a system of signs which were not pictures at all, but were more like the letters of our alphabet. They made these signs by pressing a wedge-shaped pen, or stylus, into wet clay and then allowing the clay to bake hard in the sun. From the Latin word 'cuneus', meaning a wedge, this form of writing is known as *cuneiform*. Millions of cuneiform inscriptions have been found and they have given us a vast amount of information about the ancient East.

The Sumerians were also very good at mathematics. They studied geometry and algebra as well as arithmetic. They counted by tens, just as we do. They were clever astronomers. In the clear eastern sky, which is seldom covered by clouds, the stars shine brilliantly. So the people of these countries took an interest in them from very early times. In Mesopotamia, or The Land of the Two Rivers, as the country of the Sumerians was called, the Sumerians built tall temples. They looked a little like pyramids but more like vast terraced gardens. Some scholars think that the ancestors of the Sumerians came from a mountainous land and, living as they did, on flat plains, they liked to create buildings that looked like mountains. Or perhaps these towers were first built as islands of refuge, where people fled when the floods came. They were called ziggurats. The Bible story of the building of the Tower of Babel is the story of the building of a ziggurat.

The Sumerians were a very religious people. Their priests were very powerful. It was believed that they alone knew how to persuade the gods to allow the floods to come at the proper time. The chief duty of the priests was to conduct services and ceremonies in the temples. But they were also the writers, doctors, astronomers, lawyers, scientists and artists of Sumeria.

Quite late in their history, about the year 2300 B.C., all the city states came under the control of a mighty king named Sargon. When he had finished conquering all his neighbours in the river valleys he marched his armies northwards and westwards, into the mountains. He may even have gone as far as the Mediterranean. Everywhere he found people who were civilized and were building cities.

Right: This diagram shows what a ziggurat probably looked like. The raised platforms would have protected the sanctuary from flood.

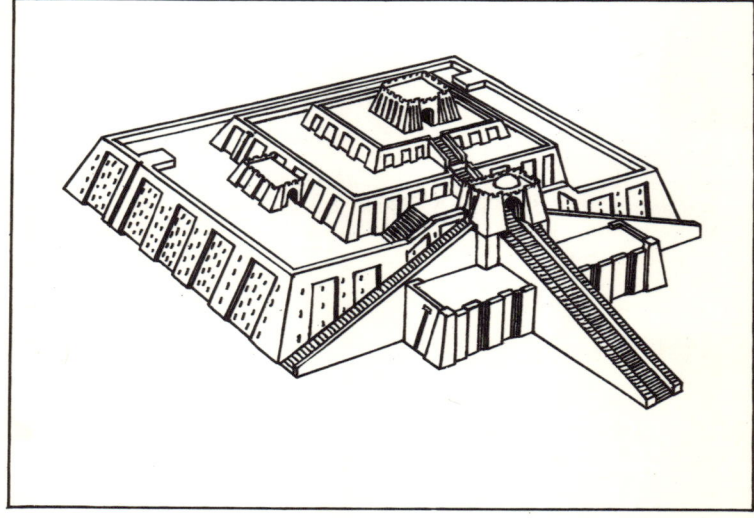

Below: The ruins of the ziggurat of Ur. Each city had its own special god, and the ziggurat could have been built to provide a dwelling place for him.

Above: The Ishtar Gate at Babylon was built during the reign of Nebuchadnezzar II (604–562 B.C.).

Left: Head of Babylonian demon, about 600 B.C.

Below: Assyrian archers.

When he died, after being king for fifty-six years, Sargon had founded one of the first of the great empires of the East. But after his death the empire soon broke up. If we look at a map again we shall see one big difference between the Nile Valley and the Fertile Crescent. The Nile Valley is protected on almost every side by the desert, but the Fertile Crescent is exposed to danger from the mountain lands to the north and east. Vigorous, warlike tribes lived in these mountains and on the plains of central Asia, beyond the mountains.

The story of Mesopotamia is, therefore, one of frequent invasions. The people of the cities in the Land of the Two Rivers would build up a fine civilization. Then, suddenly, wild tribes from the mountains would invade and destroy towns and villages. These tribes would settle and rebuild. They would build a new civilization there until, perhaps a few hundred years later, another set of wild men would invade from the hills, and the process would start all over again.

Long after the collapse of Sargon's empire, the city of Babylon created another great empire, stretching from Mesopotamia to the Mediterranean. In about 1100 B.C. the Assyrians, a people who had come from the mountains into northern Mesopotamia, destroyed Babylon and founded an empire of their own. In 612 B.C. it was the turn of the Assyrian capital city, Nineveh, to be destroyed. The people of Babylon then created a new empire that was greater than any of the previous ones.

So it went on, century after century. As the armies went farther and farther from the rivers, however, they met new peoples. One nation were the Hittites, who lived in the mountains of Asia Minor, in what is now Turkey. By 1000 B.C., they had mastered the art of smelting iron and making tools and weapons from it. Iron weapons were much stronger and harder than those made of bronze. So when the Assyrians conquered them, the Assyrians too, were able to make iron weapons, which gave them a great advantage over their enemies.

While the Hittites were still a powerful nation, the Egyptians arrived on the borders of their country. Led by a Pharaoh named Tuthmosis I (or Thothmes), the Egyptian armies marched as far as the Euphrates. Until this time the two great civilizations of the ancient world had heard about each other but had not come into contact. But from this time onwards they were in constant touch and were usually at war.

The way from the Nile valley to the Euphrates lay through the southern half of the Fertile Crescent. As we have seen, this included the lands of Palestine, Lebanon and Syria. Here, too, city states were growing up. In time, some of them joined to form kingdoms. Among the most important kingdoms were those of Syria and Israel. There were also important ports on the sea coast, the chief being Tyre and Sidon. They belonged to a seafaring nation known as the Phoenicians.

It seemed as if the people of these countries were trying to build their cities and form their states in the middle of a busy street. Armies from Egypt or Mesopotamia were constantly passing through, on the way to fight each other. Each army would demand that the cities it came upon should help with men or money. If the city refused it was besieged and destroyed. The cities used to try to side with the army they thought would win. Sometimes they were right; sometimes they were wrong. Life was exciting but dangerous in the cities of Syria and Palestine.

There was a nation among the peoples of Palestine known as the Israelites. Their chief city was Jerusalem. They said that their ancestor, Abraham, had originally come from a city of Sumeria, Ur, and had wandered, with flocks and herds, to Egypt. Later the tribe had settled in Egypt, become enslaved, and had lived there for many years. They later escaped into the desert and finally came to Palestine, where they settled and built cities.

The Israelites, or Hebrews, had different ideas about religion than most of their neighbours. While nearly all the peoples of the East worshipped a whole group of gods, who behaved much like men, the Israelites believed in one all-powerful, invisible God, who made the whole world and everything in it. They believed that they were God's chosen people.

In the Bible we read much of their story. We read of their kings and prophets and of their life in the land of Palestine all those centuries ago. We read, too, of the Assyrians and Babylonians and Egyptians and the other peoples of the ancient East. We learn about how they lived and what they thought.

The Hittites were the first people to master the art of smelting iron. Their iron weapons were much harder and stronger than those made of bronze.

Towards the end of the stories of the Old Testament we meet a new nation, the Persians. The Persians, and their neighbours the Medes, lived in the mountainous country to the east of Mesopotamia. It is still sometimes called Persia, though its modern name is Iran. When the Babylonians destroyed Nineveh, the city of the Assyrians, in the year 612 B.C. they were helped by an army of Medes.

Not many years later, the Medes and Persians were united under a great ruler named Cyrus. His armies marched into Mesopotamia and conquered the whole of the Fertile Crescent. In the other direction, they went as far as India and Central Asia. The next Persian kings extended their empire over all Asia Minor. They crossed into Europe and invaded Greece. They even conquered all Egypt. The Persian empire was the greatest the world had known at that date.

The Persian kings were good rulers. They made good laws, which were strictly enforced. Under their rule the nations of the East flourished. Farmers were able to cultivate their fields without interference from invading armies. Architects designed wonderful buildings. Weavers became expert in making garments of silk. Potters, metal-workers and all kinds of craftsmen created masterpieces of their craft.

In the end, the Persian kings over-extended themselves. The invasion of Greece was a failure. In the century ·that followed, the Greeks in turn invaded the Persian empire. We shall read how they won and how they built up a short-lived Empire even greater than that of the Persians in the next chapter.

The invasions of the Fertile Crescent still went on, though by armies from more distant countries. After the Greeks came the Romans and then, in the seventh century A.D., the Arabs. And even later, armies of wild horsemen from the plains of central Asia swept in and destroyed much of the old civilizations. These last invaders destroyed the elaborate irrigation systems, so that much of the fertile land of Mesopotamia became desert again.

Some fine examples of Persian metal work from the 6th–5th centuries B.C. The cup and the lion roundel are made of gold, the head of the ibex of bronze.

19

The Islands of the Sea

At the end of the last chapter we read of how the Persians, who had formed the greatest empire the world had known to that time, were defeated by the Greeks.

For several thousand years, the two great civilizations were those of Egypt and Mesopotamia. They were very powerful and had large armies. They had to travel along the Fertile Crescent to fight each other, and there they found other states and cities. In the mountains around the Fertile Crescent other kingdoms grew up in time and joined in the fighting. Persia itself was one of them.

Top: This map shows the extent of Greek civilization in the 7th century B.C.

Above: Young bull-leapers thrilled the Cretans at the palace of Knossos.

Right: The ruins of the palace at Knossos. The legendary minotaur, half-man, half-bull is said to have lived in the labyrinth.

Far Left: A girl on a swing. A toy dating from about 1550 B.C.

Left: A marble statuette of a priestess, about 1500 B.C.

Below: The background shows a Cretan funeral procession. The foreground shows an octopus vase and a household god.

Greece, however, is nowhere near Egypt or the Fertile Crescent. To the people who lived in the Fertile Crescent, Greece was a mysterious country across the sea, far to the west. Greeks who came to visit them voyaged by ship. They told of the islands that made up their homeland, and from the map we see that Greece does consist largely of islands and peninsulas. To the Egyptians, Babylonians and the other nations of the East, the Greeks were people who came from 'the isles of the sea'.

People who live on islands are naturally sailors. The early settlers of Greece gained much of their livelihood from fishing. They also made journeys by ship to trade with other countries across the sea. This was just as well, because Greece is a land of rocks and mountains. The soil is poor and

only a limited number of farmers could live there. They could not have supported cities.

The first great civilization of Greece grew up on the large island of Crete. It was flourishing before the year 2000 B.C. Soon afterwards Cretan sailors came to Egypt to trade. They also sailed westwards, going as far as Sicily and Spain.

These Cretans are sometimes known as Minoans, after one of their early kings, Minos. Secure on their island home, they built a wonderful civilization. Their defences were their ships, so they had no need to build strong walls. They built light, airy palaces, surrounded by beautiful gardens. The walls were painted in bright colours with lifelike pictures of people, animals and flowers. The homes of rich people even had piped water.

Centuries later, mainland Greeks remembered Crete as the home of the Minotaur. In their legends the Minotaur was a fabulous beast, half man and half bull, who demanded a tribute every nine years of youths and maidens. He lived in a great maze called the Labyrinth. Eventually he was slain by a hero named Theseus. This legend arose from confused memories of the sports which took place in the bull rings of the palace of Knossos, the chief city of Crete. Young men and girls, who were trained athletes, would enter the ring, seize a wild bull by the horns, and turn somersaults over his back! On the walls of the palace we can see paintings of them doing so.

The civilization of Crete came to an end about the year 1475 B.C., when a volcanic island in the sea north of Crete, called Thera or nowadays, Santorini, blew up. The eruption probably caused the greatest explosion ever heard by human beings. Showers of volcanic ash rained on Crete, as the island was swept by the explosion. Scores of thousands of people were killed, and the Minoan civilization never recovered.

Its place was taken by the Mycenean civilization. This was named after the people of Mycenae, a town on mainland Greece. Unlike the Minoans, the Myceneans were warlike people. They had bronze weapons, and their chiefs lived in great halls which were like the halls of the castles of the Middle Ages in Europe. They loved wearing splendid clothes and jewellery. They loved feasting in their halls, drinking wine from golden cups and listening to the songs of poets who sang to the music of the lyre.

Some of the stories they liked to hear survived long after the Mycenean civilization had disappeared. They were remembered and written down by a later Greek poet named Homer. One story describes how the Myceneans fought for the city of Troy, in Asia Minor. It is an exciting story of hand-to-hand battles between heroes and of how the Greeks managed to get into Troy by hiding inside the wooden statue of a horse. This story, as written by Homer, is known as the Iliad. Another story, called the Odyssey, describes the adventures of Odysseus on his way home to Greece at the end of the Trojan war.

The Myceneans, like the Minoans, were great sailors. They followed all the old trade routes known to the Minoans. They founded colonies as far away as Spain in the west and Cyprus in the east.

Then disaster struck. Another warlike people came into Greece, from the north and east. They were known as the Dorians. They had iron weapons, which were much stronger than the bronze weapons of the Myceneans. The Myceneans lost the war, and for three or four hundred years little is known of the story of Greece.

By about 800 B.C., a new civilization was beginning to grow up in Greece. Like civilizations in the other countries we have been reading about, it started with farmers founding villages and then towns. The Greeks stopped at this stage. Until quite late in their history, they never formed an empire or even kingdoms of any size. Each little city state was independent. It controlled only a few villages and small towns around it.

Above: The Greek cities competed in the Olympic Games every four years. The victor was crowned with a laurel wreath.

Left: The banqueting hall at Mycenae.

Most of the Greek cities, however, were on the coast. The Greeks were great sailors and traders. Even small Greek cities sent out fleets of ships to form colonies in distant countries, such as southern France, Italy, Spain and north Africa.

One of the most important of the Greek cities was Sparta. Here a group of warlike strangers had moved into the area and made slaves of the local people. These strangers formed a ruling class which governed the state very strictly. They were always prepared for warfare because they were so hated by the people who surrounded them. At the age of seven, Spartan boys were taken from their mothers and sent to schools where they learned to endure all kinds of hardship. The Spartans were very tough indeed, and they were a stern, proud race.

Above: A Spartan king.

Below: Athletes preparing for the Olympic Games. One man is scraping his skin with a bone 'strigil'. Another with long, braided hair is a boxer from Sparta.

The greatest of all the Greek cities was Athens. Life in Athens developed on very different lines from that in Sparta. The Athenians decided that they did not like being governed by a ruling class, so they worked out a system whereby every citizen had an equal share in government. It was done by casting votes. They called the system *democracy*, which means 'government by the people'.

The Greeks were great thinkers. From about 600 to 300 B.C., they created one of the most brilliant civilizations the world has ever known. Most of the ideas we have about science, politics, art and many other subjects started in Greece at this time.

When we read about these things, we generally find there was a man in ancient Greece who first studied them. Let us mention a few of them.

Hippocrates was a great doctor who founded a school of medicine.

Pythagoras and Archimedes discovered some of the laws of mathematics and physics. Anaximander studied geology and knew about fossils.

Aristotle worked out a system for classifying knowledge.

Praxiteles was a great sculptor.

Aeschylus, Sophocles and Euripedes wrote many fine plays. Plato worked out ideas for the wise ordering of government and the laws that govern social life. And one of the greatest Greeks of all, Socrates, taught his pupils how to think clearly.

Although they were so wise in many ways, the Greeks never managed to overcome the evil of war. The city states were for ever wasting their energies in fighting each other. However, there was one activity which came even before war, and that was athletics.

The Greeks were great athletes. They loved to compete with each other in such sports as racing, wrestling, jumping and throwing the javelin. They always did so entirely naked. The Greeks considered that the human body was beautiful. They loved to paint pictures and make sculptures of it. Some of the statues made by their sculptors are among the most beautiful in the world.

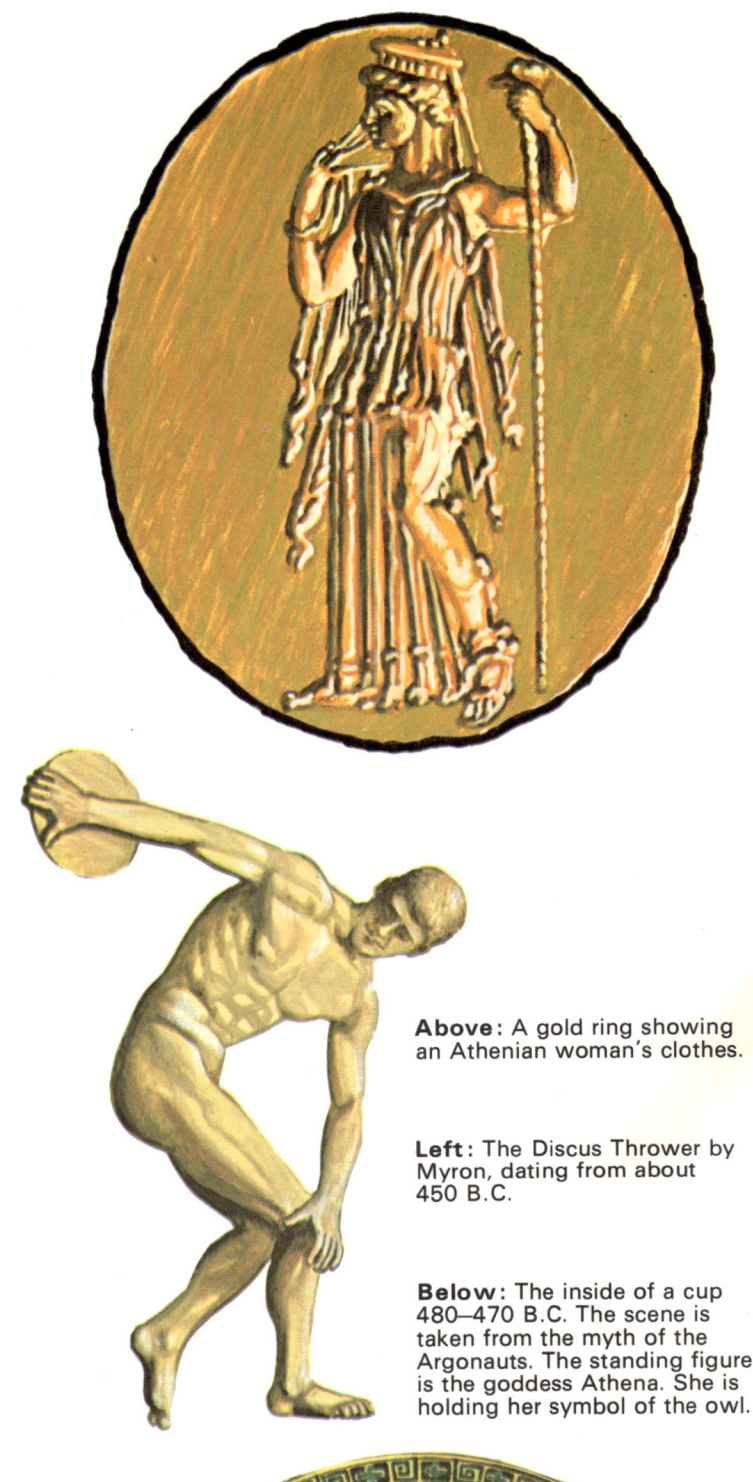

Above: A gold ring showing an Athenian woman's clothes.

Left: The Discus Thrower by Myron, dating from about 450 B.C.

Below: The inside of a cup 480–470 B.C. The scene is taken from the myth of the Argonauts. The standing figure is the goddess Athena. She is holding her symbol of the owl.

Once every four years the Greeks threw down their tools or weapons and went to Olympia for the Olympic Games. They did so even in the year 480 B.C., when the Persians were invading Greece. The Olympic Games in which athletes of all nations now take part are a revival of the ancient Greek games. The first modern Games were held in 1896.

Nowadays athletes take part usually in only one sport at a time. In ancient Greece each athlete took part in as many events as possible. The one who did best in most events was crowned victor of the Games. The following period of four years, known as the Olympiad, was named after him. But the only reward he received was a crown of laurels.

The Greeks fought a great war against the Persians, who invaded with huge armies in the year 490 B.C. and again in 480 B.C. On the first occasion the Greeks defeated their enemies in a famous battle at Marathon. News of the victory was brought to Athens by the first marathon runner, who ran for twenty-two miles to tell the news and then collapsed and died from the effort.

Ten years later the Greeks were defeated, after a tremendous battle, at Thermopylae, and the Persians captured Athens. Off the Greek coast the Athenian fleet met the Persian ships and defeated them in one of the great sea battles of history, the battle of Salamis. So the Persians, under their king Xerxes, had to retreat because their vital supply lines were broken. A Greek army finally defeated them at Plataea, near Thebes.

Some of the finest work was done by the Greek artists, scientists, writers and thinkers in the following century. But the two chief Greek states of Athens and Sparta quarrelled again and were at war with each other for twenty-seven years. In the end, their wars were stopped by the arrival of another army, from the country of Macedonia, in the north of Greece. Its king, Philip, took his army as far as Chaeronea, where he defeated the Greeks. He forced an alliance on them and the independence of the Greek city states was at an end.

Left: A copy of the Cnidian Venus by Praxiteles. The original, made about 350 B.C., has been lost. This Venus had her sanctuary on the island of Cnidos and for five hundred years boat-loads of pilgrims came to see her.

Below: The west porch of the Erechtheum on the Acropolis at Athens.

Below Right: The inside of a cup, 520–510 B.C. The cup is signed by Epictetus whose name means 'slave'.

His son, Alexander, who was only seventeen when his father died, decided to put his father's plan into practice and invade Asia. He crossed into Asia Minor and for eleven years led a victorious army into almost every part of the known world. He conquered Egypt. He defeated the Persian king and chased him through Mesopotamia and far into central Asia. He led his Greeks into countries that they had never heard of before, into what is now Afghanistan, Turkestan and Pakistan. He crossed into India and defeated the Indian king beyond the river Indus. He founded new cities everywhere, calling most of them Alexandria. Eventually, he came back to the Land of the Two Rivers and died in Babylon. He was thirty-two years old when he died, and he had created the greatest empire that his world had known.

Above: Head of Alexander, from a mosaic of the 4th century B.C. This is part of a famous mosaic showing the battle of Issus where Alexander first defeated Darius, king of Persia.

Left: Part of a Greek vase, showing Apollo. He was just and wise and ever youthful. Apollo was the Greek god of medicine, music and prophecy.

Alexander had a vision of creating an empire across the world, in which Greeks and other peoples mixed on equal terms. After he died, however, his generals quarrelled among themselves. Some of the most powerful carved out kingdoms for themselves from the conquered countries.

From that time onwards, there were Greeks everywhere in the eastern world, for most of Alexander's soldiers settled there and never returned to Greece. Greek became the universal language. One of Alexander's cities, Alexandria in Egypt, became the largest and most magnificient city in the world. But Greece itself lost its importance and was soon to be conquered by the Romans.

The City on the Seven Hills

Look at the map again and you will see that we are moving westward. Our first chapters dealt with eastern countries. Then, from the Fertile Crescent, we leaped west to the isles of Greece. Now we move further to the west and arrive in Italy.

Early Greek sailors discovered Italy by sailing west across the Ionian sea. They founded colonies there, and the Greeks who lived there traded with farmers and miners who lived inland. They bought wheat, leather, gold, farm animals, olive oil and sent them back to Greece.

Most of their colonies were in southern Italy. In central Italy, a civilized people called the Etruscans had built towns and formed city states, just like the Greeks had done. They had comfortable houses and were clever artists. They had invented a form of writing, but we do not yet know how to read it.

The Etruscan cities, like those of the Greeks, often made war against each other. They were governed by kings.

In the year 753 B.C. a group of settlers under a leader named Romulus founded a city by the river Tiber. They called it Rome. It soon spread over seven hills on the left bank of the river. The highest and steepest of the hills was known as the Capitol. There the people built a temple and a fort, where they could take refuge when danger threatened. This was the centre of what later became the greatest city in the world.

The Roman Empire reached its greatest extent under the Emperor Trajan A.D. 98–117.

Above: An Etruscan woman.

Right: A Roman necklace in gold, with emeralds and mother-of-pearl. It was made in the first century B.C. and found in Pompeii.

Right: An Etruscan funeral urn from Vulci, 9th–8th centuries B.C. The Etruscans built their early tombs like houses. Some had everything needed for the after-life carved on their walls.

Below: An Etruscan flute player, from a wall-painting in a tomb at Tarquinia. The fact that women feasted with men and played a more important part in society would have scandalised the Greeks.

Very early on, the Romans built a bridge over the river Tiber. It was a very important bridge, because most of the trade between south and north Italy had to pass over it. As a result, Rome became an important trading city in central Italy.

At first Rome was governed by Etruscan kings. But in the year 509 B.C. the Romans rebelled and chased them away. From that time on, they governed themselves and formed a republic. Two important men were elected each year to serve as consuls. The consuls ruled the city, with the help of a group of people known as the senate. The consuls only served for one year. At first, members of leading families were the only people who could stand for election to the senate. Later, the ordinary people rebelled against this idea, so, after a lot of trouble, they were allowed to vote, too.

Gradually, the power of the Etruscan kings in Italy declined. They were defeated in battles by the Greek colonists. So the other cities of Italy began to look to Rome as their leader. By about 300 B.C. the Romans controlled most of central and southern Italy.

The Romans were a different type of people from the Greeks. The Greeks were lively, gay and artistic. The Romans were stern and rather solemn people. They were honest and fair and lived good lives. They loved their children but brought them up strictly.

The Romans were great engineers and architects. They were wonderful organizers and Roman law is still the basis of the legal systems of many countries in Europe and Latin America. They also did important work in the field of literature and language, although their contributions in science were not so impressive.

In the chapter on The Fertile Crescent we read about the cities of Tyre and Sidon. They were sea-ports on the eastern shores of the Mediterranean, where the Phoenicians lived. The Phoenicians were great sailors. Their ships went trading to the farthest end of the Mediterranean and even went through the Straits of Gibraltar to the countries beyond. The Phoenicians formed many colonies, the greatest being Carthage. When Alexander the Great conquered Tyre, Carthage became the head of the Phoenician empire.

At first the war between Carthage and Rome was a strange one. Carthage was a sea empire, whereas the Romans were not good sailors. Some of the first battles were fought in Spain, where both Rome and Carthage had colonies. Then Hannibal, a great Carthaginian general, formed a huge army in Spain and marched it through southern France and across the Alps into Italy. He even took elephants with him over the Alpine passes. His army stayed in Italy for fourteen years, capturing many towns, but Hannibal never succeeded in capturing Rome itself.

Meanwhile, the Romans landed an army in North Africa under its general, Scipio. After a time, this army threatened Carthage itself. The Carthaginians were forced to send for Hannibal. He returned from Italy but was defeated by Scipio in a great battle. Carthage was beaten, and Rome became the most powerful state in the world.

The end of Carthage came in the year 146 B.C. Within the next two hundred years, the Romans conquered almost all of the known world. Every country bordering the Mediterranean sea belonged to them. There were Roman armies and Roman governors in Egypt, Palestine, Asia Minor, Greece and Spain. One of the greatest Roman generals, Julius Caesar, conquered the whole of France, which was then known as Gaul. In A.D. 43 Roman armies invaded Britain. Not long afterwards they marched through Armenia to the shores of the Caspian sea and down through Mesopotamia to the Persian Gulf.

Above: A Roman coin showing an elephant.

Left: Julius Caesar left a fascinating account of his campaign in Gaul. He finally overcame the Gauls in the great battle of Alesia when he defeated Vercingetorix.

Above: A Roman butcher's shop. Notice how the joints are displayed in an orderly way.

Far Left: Julius Caesar 100—44 B.C.

Left: A gold ring with an engraved portrait. Made in the first century B.C., it was found in the house of Menander, Pompeii.

There had never been such a vast and powerful state in the world before. At the height of its power, more than 100,000,000 people were living in it. The old idea of a republic, however, had been altered. The senate and the consuls were still elected, but the emperor was placed above them. In Shakespeare's play, *Julius Caesar*, we read how the great general, Julius Caesar, was murdered by a group of republicans when it seemed that he would accept the title of emperor. Twelve years after Caesar's death, his nephew, Octavian, became in fact, the first Roman emperor in 29 B.C. In 27 B.C. the Senate gave him the name of Augustus.

The Roman army consisted of about thirty legions. Each legion had between 3,000 and 6,000 men. They were all superbly trained soldiers. In addition to fighting wars with tribes who lived beyond the Roman frontiers, they kept order in the countries which Rome controlled.

The Romans were strict but just. They made fair laws and were quite merciless to people who broke them. Above all, the Romans gave peace to the world. For several hundred years, the people who lived in the countries around the Mediterranean could engage in trade or art and enjoy life without fear of invading armies. This was called the *Pax Romana*, the Roman Peace.

We have seen how the ordinary people of Rome won the right to vote in elections. For a time, only the people who lived in Rome could do so. But, as the Empire grew, so many other people were given the right to call themselves Roman citizens. It was a right that was greatly prized. No-one who was a Roman citizen could be punished by any other court than a Roman one. A man knew that in a Roman court the law would be strictly observed. In the New Testament Paul demanded the right to be sent to Rome for trial, because he was a Roman citizen.

31

Any citizen could rise to the highest office in the Empire At first the emperors were pure-bred Romans, but later there were emperors who had been born in other countries, such as Spain, Austria and Britain. There was a wide exchange of people in all parts of the Roman world. A Syrian might find himself serving in the army in northern Britain. When his period of service was over he might settle there on a farm granted to him by the government. Similarly, a Briton might settle in Syria. In this way, men with military experience settled the outposts of the empire.

There were dark sides to the Roman civilization. The worst was the existence of slavery. At least one-third of the people in the Roman empire were slaves. Some were born as slaves, some were sold into slavery for debt or for crime, but most were prisoners captured in wars. Some slaves were well treated, especially those who worked in private houses or on farms. Others were cruelly treated, especially those who worked in mines or pulled the oars of galleys. One of the reasons why the Roman world did not make as much progress as we have made in the past two hundred years is that there was no reason for anyone to invent machinery. There were always plenty of slaves to do the work.

Another feature of Roman life which we would find shocking were the games. They started when Rome was a small town. People enjoyed games and sports at annual fairs and fêtes. There were also funeral games, held in honour of important people who had died. The Greeks had games like this, in which athletes took part. The Greek athletes were amateurs, who took part because they loved to do so, but the athletes who took part in Etruscan and Roman games were paid performers.

As time went on, the games became more and more bloodthirsty. It was as if the people who go nowadays to see a boxing match were not content to see one of the boxers knocked down. Instead, they would want to see him killed. Roman boxers fought in metal gloves, with sharp spikes on them.

Above: The Roman Forum as it is today. The temple of Saturn is in the foreground, and the Senate house to the left.

Left: A slave's label. 'Hold me lest I escape and send me back to my master Viventius on the estate of Callistus.'

Below: A haggler in an open-air market.

Left: Venus chastising Cupid from a fresco in Pompeii.

Left: Scene's from a boy's life. A newly born child was held by his father in token of support. This goes back to the days when Romans killed unwanted children.

Below: Slaves were specially trained as gladiators. Here *Myrmillo* with sword and helmet meets *Retiarius* with net and trident in a duel to the death.

In almost every Roman city a large open-air theatre was built. There were rows and rows of seats rising in tiers around a central arena. Battles, not plays, were staged here. The men who fought each other in these battles were known as gladiators. Sometimes they fought with swords, spears and daggers; sometimes a man with a sword would be matched against a man with a fishing-net and a fisherman's trident. Often full-scale battles with hundreds of men on either side took place, or gladiators would be matched against wild animals. In Rome itself, sometimes several thousand animals were killed in one day in a huge theatre show. Most of the wild animals in North Africa were caught and taken to Rome for slaughter in the arenas.

Criminals were also driven into the arenas to be eaten by wild animals while the crowds watched. Many Christians met their deaths in this way. For three hundred years, they were regarded as criminals by the Roman government. This was chiefly because the Romans thought so highly of their empire that they considered the Emperor divine. He was a god and had to be honoured as a god. The Christians refused to do this, and so they were persecuted, thrown into prison and killed.

In the end, Christianity triumphed. The Empire was growing old and tired. People were having to pay too much of their money in taxes. Officials were asking for bribes. The old Roman virtues of being honest, fair and true were forgotten. There were more slaves than ever. Many strange kinds of religion flourished. And beyond the frontiers of the Roman empire, especially in the forests of central Europe, wild, warlike tribes were hovering, awaiting their chance to attack and plunder.

Peace came at last to the Christians in the year A.D. 313, and Constantine became the first Christian emperor twenty-five years later. Before long the leader of the Christian Church, the Pope in Rome, was, next to the Emperor, the most important man in the Roman world.

Above: A girl from Pompeii pauses for a moment. She is holding a *stilus* and a wax tablet or *tabella*.

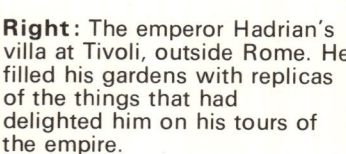

Right: The emperor Hadrian's villa at Tivoli, outside Rome. He filled his gardens with replicas of the things that had delighted him on his tours of the empire.

Meanwhile, the tribes from beyond the Roman frontiers formed large armies and began to invade the empire. They crossed into France. They invaded Greece. And in the year A.D. 410 they captured Rome itself. The people of the Roman world could hardly believe that Rome, 'the Eternal City', had been taken by her enemies.

Roman emperors continued to try to govern for a few more years. The last became emperor in the year A.D. 476. From that time, the empire was governed from a new city, Constantinople, which we now know as Istanbul, in Turkey.

The city of Rome survived, however. With no emperor living there, the Pope became very powerful—as powerful as the emperor had been As new nations grew up in Europe, their kings looked to the Pope as their leader—or 'father', because the title 'Pope' really means 'father'. The kings of France, Spain, England, Germany and other countries were all independent, but during the Middle Ages they looked to the Pope as their spiritual leader. In all these countries, the laws were based on Roman laws. Many of them spoke languages derived from Latin and they still used the great legacy of the Empire—the Roman roads. Many of these roads still survive and we can travel on them today.

Above: The Romans caught most of the animals in North Africa, for the arenas of the Roman empire. This scene of an animal hunt is taken from a mosaic of the 4th century A.D. found in North Africa.

Right: A Roman priest. In 65 B.C. Caesar became Pontifex Maximus and used his position as head of the college of priests to further his own ambitions.

Far Right: A capital from the great Byzantine church of Santa Sofia in Constantinople. After the fall of Constantinople in 1453, Santa Sofia became a mosque. Now it is a museum.

India

Back to the map again. We have now travelled as far to the west as we can go without crossing the Atlantic ocean. The Roman Empire included the whole Atlantic coast of Europe, from Morocco to northern Britain. Now we return to the East.

Beyond the Fertile Crescent and the mountains and deserts of Persia, lies the enormous country of India. We have visited it once with the armies of Alexander the Great, who defeated an Indian army beyond the river Indus. The Romans never conquered India but they knew about it. Traders went, mostly by ship, to both the west and east coasts of India and also to Ceylon (now known as Sri Lanka). They brought back spices, silks, peacocks, precious stones and other valuable goods to be sold in Roman markets.

When Alexander arrived in India, he found a civilized land. India had been civilized for thousands of years.

Above: Head of a bearded man. Made in stone, this could be a god or a king. Found in Mohenjo-Daro, this dates from about 3000 B.C.

Above Right: A scene from life in Mohenjo-Daro. The building in the background is a granary, and the beautiful head-dresses and jewellery of the women is taken from clay figures of the period.

Left: A map to show the three great rivers of India, where the early civilizations began.

Northern India is a land of great rivers. The two most important are the Indus and the Ganges. What happened in the lands beside these rivers was very similar to what happened by those other rivers we have read about, the Euphrates, the Tigris and the Nile. Men settled by the banks of the Indus and Ganges from very early times and built villages and towns. They made irrigation channels to use the water and mud of the rivers for feeding the growing crops. States and kingdoms were formed from their settlements and towns.

Looking at the map, we see that India is like a great triangle, pointing south. In the north, it is cut off from central Asia by an immense range of mountains. These are the Himalayas, which include Everest, the highest mountain on earth. The two great rivers of India, and a third known as the Brahmaputra, rise in the Himalayas. The Indus flows south-westwards to the Arabian sea. The Ganges and Brahmaputra flow south-eastwards and southwards to

the Bay of Bengal. These great river valleys lie farther south than those of the Tigris and Euphrates. They are also protected from north winds by the mountains.

There are, however, passes through these mountains, although they are so high. Most of these passes are found in the north-west. Adventurous people from central Asia who are willing to brave the snow and ice can find their way into India. The story of ancient India is largely a story of invaders who have come into the country by this route.

We do not know where the first settlers in India came from, but by about the year 2500 B.C. they had created a civilization in the Indus valley. They built large cities with buildings of mud bricks, with stone foundations. Their weapons and tools were made of copper. They were skilful at making pottery, which they decorated with brightly coloured patterns and with pictures of birds and animals. They had invented the wheel and used it in their bullock carts.

They had also developed a system of writing, based on pictures. Many inscriptions have been found, chiefly on seals and bricks, but we have not yet learned how to read them.

Two of the chief towns of this early civilization in the Indus valley were Harappa and Mohenjo-Daro. Harappa is about 160 kilometres south-west of the modern city of Lahore. Mohenjo-Daro is about 320 kilometres north of Karachi in Pakistan. They were very large cities, with many hectares of streets laid out around a protecting citadel. The mounds which mark the site of Mohenjo-Daro cover a square with sides of about 1.6 kilometres. Much of the city consisted of streets of little brick houses, all alike, in which either slaves or very poor people probably lived.

The people of the Indus valley discovered how to use cotton. They learned to weave cotton fibre and to dye the cloth from it. They traded their cloth with the Sumerians, who were living in the Land of the Two Rivers at the same time. Probably the trade was carried on by merchants who lived in the lands between India and Mesopotamia. This area is now barren desert, but we think it had a better climate in those days. Some Harappa traders, however, seem to have settled in Sumerian cities and worked there.

The cities of the Indus valley were abandoned about the year 1750 B.C. There is evidence of flooding at that time, but we do not know if the floods were caused by a national disaster or by neglect. The young men could have been away fighting invaders.

During this period, new nations were migrating through the mountain passes and spreading over all India. They were people from central Asia, and they were known as the Aryans. Their chief wealth was their cattle, and they were not nearly as civilized as the people who lived in the Indus valley cities. But they brought one new thing with them that was almost unknown in India—the horse.

The Aryans used war chariots when they charged their enemies. This must have

Right: These Indian seals were made in Mohenjo-Daro between 2000 and 3000 B.C.

Right: A peacock medallion from the second century B.C., made in one of the settlements on the river Ganges.

Below: A statue of Yakshi, from Sanchi in Central India, 1st century A.D.

terrified the Indus valley people, who could only reply with slow-moving bullock carts —no match for fast, quick-turning horses.

Our knowledge of the people who lived in the Indus valley cities comes chiefly from discoveries made by scholars digging in the ruins of their homes. However, we learn much more about the Aryans from the books they have left behind. There are four chief books, known as the Vedas, which are the holy books of the Hindus today. They tell of how the Aryan heroes who invaded India lived and fought. We can read of the songs they sang and of their thoughts and ideas.

The Aryans settled down in the Indian villages as chiefs and nobles. The people who were there before them became either slaves or poor peasants. They were expected to do all the work which the Aryans did not like to do. The caste-system which we know in India today grew up from this arrangement. Every man does the same sort of work as his father did. If his father was a priest, so is he. If his father was only a road-sweeper, he can never hope to be anything else. No man can ever move up to a higher place in society.

The system caused much unrest and discontent. About the year 560 B.C. a prince of a tribe living just south of the Himalayas rebelled against it. He went away from home and thought about the problem for more than six years. Then he came back and began preaching. His name was Gautama. Soon he was known as Buddha, which means 'The Enlightened One'. He taught that all the suffering in the world is caused by greed. A man should, therefore, turn his back on the idea of trying to get things for himself, and in this way he would gain happiness.

Below: The Prince setting forth on his journey towards enlightenment, from a relief of the second century A.D.

Above: The calm, serene face of Buddha. From the fifth century A.D., this sandstone statue comes from Mathura, India.

For about two hundred years Buddhism, the religion founded by Buddha, was confined to a smallish area of north-east India. Then a ruler named Asoka conquered the region. When he learned about Buddhism he became sorry for all the evil he had caused by his wars. So he became a Buddhist and made it the chief religion of his empire, which included most of India.

Asoka was emperor from 264 to 223 B.C. In an earlier chapter we read of how Alexander the Great invaded north-west India in 327 B.C. Alexander founded many new cities and states in Asia and left Greek colonies in them. Asoka decided to send missionaries to preach Buddhism in these countries. So there was much interchange of thought and ideas between East and West.

Above: The north gate of a Buddhist stupa at Sanchi.

Left: The birth of Buddha. He is represented as the support of the Universe, (from Nepal about A.D. 1000.)

Far Left: Embroidery from a court coat of a Moghul prince or emperor, from the first half of the seventeenth century.

Below: A Buddhist stupa at Sanchi. Every detail is symbolic, for example, the dome represents the heavens enclosing the earth.

For a time most of the people of India remained Buddhist. Then the Hindu priests persuaded many of them to return to the old Hindu religion. For centuries the two religions competed with each other. But in the end the Hindu religion won back most of India, and Buddhism moved to China, Burma, Ceylon and many other eastern countries.

After the time of Asoka, India was divided among numerous small kingdoms for several centuries. And it was at this time that the Christian religion arrived. It is supposed to have been taken there by the apostle Thomas. He landed at a Roman trading settlement at Madras and was killed. There is still a Christian church in south India which is supposed to have been founded by him.

Another important Indian empire began soon after the year A.D. 300. Its most important king was called Chandragupta II. In the peaceful years when this empire flourished many splendid works of art were produced by Indian painters and sculptors. Rich people lived in comfort and luxury. Scientists and scholars were also at work. They worked out new systems of mathematics, and some of them seem to have known that the earth was round and that it revolved around the sun.

This empire was destroyed by another invasion of wild people who came through the mountain passes. Then, after the year A.D. 700, the followers of the prophet Mohammed arrived in India to found new kingdoms and spread a new religion.

For several centuries Mohammedanism, or Islam, was spread by the Arabs. Mohammed was, of course, an Arab, who had lived in Arabia. Then, soon after the year 1200, an army of people known as Mongols, from central Asia, swept over the passes and settled in northern India. They founded a great empire, the Moghul Empire, which was one of the most magnificent India had ever known. It lasted for several hundred years and was still flourishing when the first Europeans found their way by sea to India.

Top Left: A Moghul miniature, showing the exquisite painting of the period.

Above: Moghul sword hilt in the shape of a horse's head. It is made of jade and is encrusted with precious stones and inlaid with gold. Swords like this are often seen in the miniatures of the period.

Left: A text from the Koran, the holy book of Islam.

China

Eastwards, far beyond India, lies an even vaster country—China. Look at the map and you will see that to reach it from India you would have either to cross many high mountain ranges or to sail for thousands of miles around south-east Asia. From Europe the journey is even greater. More high mountains and immense deserts bar the way. In the thirteenth century one of the first Europeans to visit China, Marco Polo, took four years to make the journey. Even now, if you were to walk all the way, it would take you just as long.

Like India and Mesopotamia, China has two great rivers. They are among the longest, deepest and broadest rivers in the world, much larger than even the Indus and the Ganges. Their names are the Yangtze-kiang and the Hoang-ho. The Yangtze-kiang flows through the central part of China; the Hoang-ho through the north. Both flow eastwards across China into the China sea.

Events in early China were much the same as in Egypt, Mesopotamia and India. Men who had been hunters settled down to farm on the banks of the rivers. They grew their crops in the rich mud laid down by the rivers. They built villages and towns. The towns combined to form states. All this was happening at the same time as the Sumerians and the Egyptians were forming their own cities, states and empires in Mesopotamia and Egypt.

We do not know as much as we would like about the early history of China because of the actions of an emperor who lived about 200 B.C. He was the emperor of one of the Chinese states called Ch'in. That is where the name 'China' comes from. The Ch'in people conquered most of their neighbours and in that way united most of China. Their emperor called himself Ch'in Shih Huang Ti, which means 'the first emperor of Ch'in'. He was a very vain man. His courtiers persuaded him that he was more important than he really was. 'No-one else who is worth remembering has ever lived before you,' they told him. Ch'in Shih Huang Ti agreed. 'History begins with me,' he said. And so he destroyed all the old records and history books and statues of people who had lived before him.

He did not live long, and so some records escaped. But so many were destroyed that we do not know as much about ancient China as we might have done.

From the surviving records we learn that there were civilized kingdoms in China well before 1600 B.C. The people who lived in them knew how to make bronze. They had also invented a kind of picture writing. They wrote mostly on strips of bamboo tied together, and also on silk.

Above: A bronze vessel from the 13th–12th centuries B.C. It was used to hold the fragrant wine which was offered to the ancestors, and was decorated with magic symbols.

Left: This map shows the two great rivers of China, the Hoang-ho and the Yangtze-kiang.

Right: Kuan Ti, the Chinese god of war and literature. He was a god who could avoid war and uphold justice.

42

Silk was one of the things discovered by the early Chinese. It is made from the silky cocoon which protects the chrysalis of the silk moth. The Chinese learned how to feed the silk moth caterpillars on mulberry leaves, then how to unwind the silk and to use it for weaving into a delicate cloth. Silk was valued very highly, and rolls of silk were even used for money. By Roman times, some was carried right across Asia to the West, where it commanded enormous prices. The western peoples, who made their clothes from linen and wool, had never seen anything as fine.

The Chinese also became expert in carving jade. Jade is a shiny precious stone, usually pale green in colour. The Chinese thought it even more valuable than gold.

About the time that Buddha was teaching in India, a wise man named Kung Futzu, or Confucius, began to teach in China. He said that it was wrong for certain men to be princes and rulers simply because they had been born into certain families. He taught that everyone should have an equal chance to do what he was able to do. At school everyone should be taught as many subjects as possible, to find out what he was good at. In Confucius's school the pupils were taught racing and archery as well as reading and arithmetic.

To find out who was best, the scholars were given examinations. When the teaching of Confucius became widely followed in China, it was impossible for anyone to get any sort of job with the government without taking examinations. Many of the Chinese seemed to spend most of their lives taking examinations. Those who were successful in examinations were treated with great respect, as were all old people.

About the same time another teacher, whose name is unknown, tried to lead the Chinese back to a simple life. He said they should leave the artificial life of the towns and go and live in the country, to study nature. His creed is called Taoism. Many artists and writers followed it and were inspired to make wonderful works of art. Chinese painting in particular is very lovely. It is often done on silk.

When Ch'in Shih Huang Ti became emperor he faced invasion from the north. Wild horsemen from the plains of central Asia created havoc wherever they went. He built a great wall, in order to protect his country from these damaging raids. It was one of the greatest building works ever undertaken by men. It contains many, many more tonnes of stones than the Pyramids. It is more than 2410 kilometres long, and for much of the way it is wide enough to carry a road along the top. It is called The Great Wall of China. Sentries marched along it, to keep watch over the hills and plains beyond.

Not long after the death of Ch'in Shih Huang Ti a new family of emperors began to rule China. They were known as the Han emperors. They controlled China for four hundred years. They built great cities, produced many wonderful works of art, irrigated enormous areas of land with canals, and made important inventions.

Paper was invented during this period. The Chinese discovered how to make paper about the year A.D. 105. Europeans did not learn the secret until more than a thousand years later. It came to Europe by way of the Arabs, who had learned it from the Chinese. Before this date, Europeans had written on papyrus and parchment.

During the second century A.D., the Chinese discovered the magnetic compass. It was discovered that a magnetic needle always pointed towards the north. They did not, however, use the compass for guiding ships at sea. Many years passed before they realized how useful it could be for that purpose.

The Chinese had ships large and sturdy enough to make very long voyages. Some of the ships had three or four decks and were as much as 120 metres long. They carried great square sails and were known as junks. Chinese sailors voyaged in these boats as far as India, East Africa and even Egypt. The Chinese invented a new way of steering a boat, by means of a rudder. They also learned to use a paddle-wheel in small boats.

Above Right: Chinese merchants travelling in a caravan across central Asia.

Right: Pottery figure of a lady, from the T'ang dynasty (A.D. 618–906).

Above: A lute, inlaid with mother-of-pearl, amber and tortoiseshell. It belonged to an emperor of the 8th century, and shows the luxury of the court life of the period.

Right: The great wall of China.

During the time of the Han emperors Buddhism began to be preached in China, and many of the people eventually became Buddhists.

We have already read about the *Pax Romana*, the Roman Peace. The Han Empire was flourishing in China at the same time, and trade grew up between the two empires. The traders travelled the long, long route across the deserts, mountains and plains of central Asia. They travelled in caravans—groups of people, with their animals, goods and often their families, all travelling together. Many of the goods were carried on the backs of camels. They used the two-humped Bactrian camels, with long brown hair. Chinese merchants were to be seen selling their goods, such as silk, jade, porcelain and gold, in the markets of Asia Minor, Mesopotamia and Syria. Greek traders, whose home was in the Roman Empire, travelled as far as the cities of China. Merchants from the two empires also met in the ports of India, Ceylon and the Red Sea.

Above: A jade *tsung*, symbol of the square earth. A Tsung was put on the stomach of the deceased during burial.

Left: A Chinese watch-tower. Made in green glazed pottery it dates from the Han dynasty (206 B.C. – A.D. 220).

After the collapse of the Han and Roman empires, wild, uncivilized men broke in, and for centuries trade ceased. But it started again early in the thirteenth century.

The Mongols were the last of the savage peoples who swept into both Europe and China from the plains of central Asia. We read about them in a previous chapter. Their leaders were among the greatest conquerors the world has ever known. In the year A.D. 1211 they invaded and conquered north China. Then they turned westwards. Their armies poured into all the countries of the Fertile Crescent and even came as far as central Germany.

At first they destroyed everything and killed many people. Then they settled down. The Mongols were good at organization and they founded an immense empire, which stretched from the Pacific ocean right across Asia to the Mediterranean sea. There was peace throughout these vast territories. So once again traders were able to travel backwards and forwards between China and Europe.

One of the first travellers to do so was an Italian named Marco Polo. He travelled right across Asia to China, the journey taking four years. In China he met the great Mongol emperor, Kublai Khan. This great emperor was impressed by Marco Polo and gave him a great deal of responsible work to do. He sent him on errands to many places in south-east Asia. Marco Polo became a very important person in China. The Emperor wanted him to stay in China all his life, but after many years Marco became homesick. He wanted to see Italy again. So he travelled home by sea.

Back at home his neighbours nicknamed him 'Marco Millions', because he was always talking about millions. Millions of people, millions of pounds of money, millions of kilometres, millions of ships. When Marco showed them some of the treasures he had brought home, people began to understand about the marvellous land he had visited, so far away.

When the Mongols invaded China in the thirteenth century, they found it prosperous under a family, or dynasty, of emperors

Above: Plate and cup from the Hsüan Te period (1426–1435).

Right: A reconstruction of Su Sung's clock about 1090. This clock-tower was more than ten metres high. It was operated by water-power and every quarter of an hour there would be a great sound of creaking and splashing, clanging and ringing.

Left: The arrival of Portuguese merchants in Japan in 1542. Accompanied by missionaries, these men aroused great interest and curiosity in Japan about the manners and customs of the Western world.

known as the Sung. Their capital city was Hangchow. It had over a million people living in it, which made it easily the largest city in the world at that time. Situated by a broad river, it had canals instead of streets. It was a city of shops, gardens and comfortable houses.

By this time the Chinese had made many discoveries and inventions that were unknown in Europe. They had learned how to print on paper. They even had printed bank-notes. This was completely unknown in Europe.

Gunpowder was another new invention from this period. At first it was used only for making fireworks. The Chinese are very fond of firework displays at feasts and festivals. Later it was used in weapons. The Chinese then made guns, bombs, hand grenades and rockets.

They had factories for making all kinds of metal goods. Iron was common, and they used coal for smelting it and also for heating their houses. They had fine clocks, worked by water. In making and decorating porcelain, they had become very expert indeed. Look at some Chinese porcelain in a museum and see how lovely it is.

From that time, Europeans never forgot China. They quickly learned the secrets of making gunpowder, of using silk and of printing. They were eager to trade with China. It was in the hope of reaching India and China that Christopher Columbus sailed westward in 1492 and discovered America instead.

Right: The Phoenix Hall at Uji near Kyoto. This beautiful temple was built in 1053 and it takes its name from the bronze figures on the roof.

The Barbarians

From the very earliest times people who have lived in cities and civilized states have never felt very secure. They have known always that beyond the limits of their own city or country there lived wild men who might invade at any time. So their kings and rulers formed armies to protect them.

Usually the armies failed. Sooner or later the wild men poured over the frontiers. At first they killed and destroyed everything. Then they settled down and built up a new civilization. In its turn, this was destroyed by a new wave of wild invaders. History is mostly a record of new beginnings.

In the previous chapters we have met many instances of such events. The story of the Fertile Crescent is one of frequent invasions. Even Egypt, almost surrounded by deserts, was invaded by the people known as 'The Shepherd Kings'. And the great Roman Empire fell at last to savage invaders from the north.

The Romans and Greeks called the people who lived outside their countries 'barbarians'. They were really laughing at them, because they could not speak Greek or Latin. 'Ha-ha,' they said, 'all that these savages can say is "bar-bar"!' So they called them 'barbarians'.

The name 'barbarians' was used for any uncivilized people. Wandering Arabs who lived in the deserts were barbarians. So were the savage Picts who roamed over the mountains of Scotland. However, most of the barbarians who attacked the civilized world came from central Asia.

Central Asia is a vast region. There are great deserts, huge lakes, high mountain ranges and immense plains.

The people who live here have always been herdsmen. The animals they kept included sheep, cattle, goats, horses and camels. Many of these tribes lived a nomadic life. They simply followed their animals wherever they went over the vast plains. In winter they lived on the lower land; in summer they went up into the mountains.

Below: The Hyksos invade Egypt. These people known as the 'Shepherd Kings' attacked the Egyptian armies with horse-drawn chariots.

It seems that the plains of central Asia have been drying up over the past few thousand years. The lakes have been shrinking, and much countryside that was formerly grassland is now desert. As this has happened, there has been less grass for the animals to eat and the tribes have wandered farther and farther in their search for grazing. They have wandered on to land which other tribes have regarded as their own. Then the two tribes have fought.

Usually the invading tribe has won. Then the losers have moved away to the grazing lands of yet another tribe. Soon the whole region was filled with tribes moving and fighting each other.

These movements reached tribes living on the borders of civilized lands. On the one side they were harassed by other tribes, wanting to move into their grazing land. On the other, they were able to see cultivated fields, houses, cities and other treasures. So they formed an army and swept into the rich, civilized lands.

Events like these took place long before man began to write history. Scholars have learned about them through excavating the remains of ancient cities. In some places, especially in the Fertile Crescent, they have found the remains of ten or fifteen cities built one on top of the other. Each one was destroyed by a new wave of invaders, who later built another city on the same site.

In many instances, the invaders have been helped by having better weapons or better methods of warfare than the civilized people. On page 23 we read how the invading Dorians had iron weapons, whereas the people they fought, the Mycenean Greeks, had bronze. The same thing happened, time and again. Later in this chapter we read of how the Huns worked out a system of attack which bewildered their enemies.

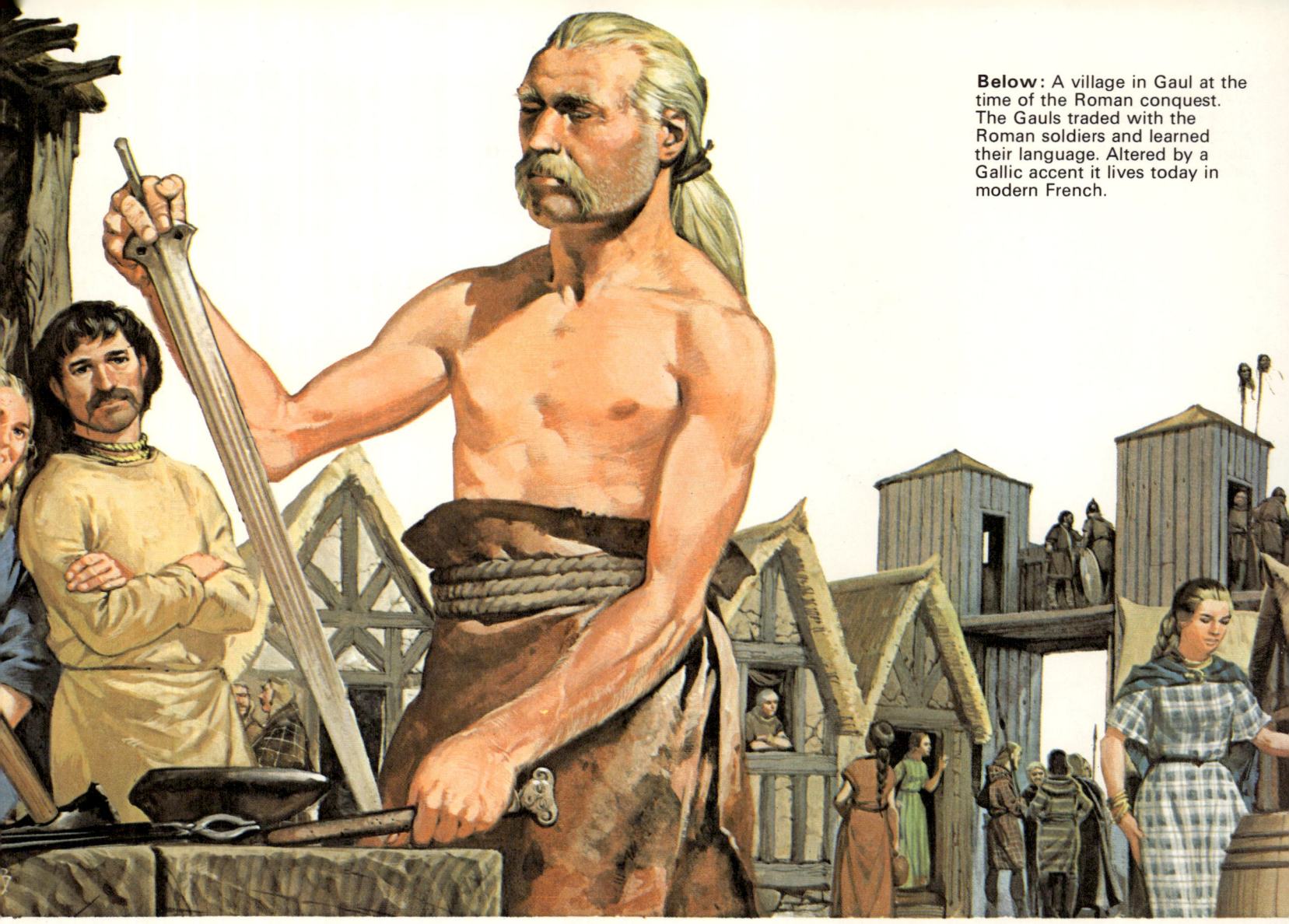

One of the first big invasions to affect Europe was that of the Celts. The Celts started to move into the countries north of the Mediterranean about the year 650 B.C. They were a tall, golden-haired people, who loved fine clothes and ornaments. The men wore long, flowing moustaches and long hair. They loved fighting and feasting. Around their camp-fires at night they loved to hear poets sing of the mighty deeds of heroes. Their smiths were skilful in working both bronze and iron. They were just beginning to use coins, and they had also learned how to make glass.

The Celts were responsible for making most of the hill forts, now covered with grass, which we see in Britain and other parts of western Europe. Some of them were very cleverly designed. Mostly, however, the Celts preferred to fight in the open, often from chariots drawn by horses.

Immense numbers of Celtic tribes invaded western Europe between the years 600 and 200 B.C. In 390 B.C. they poured into Italy and burnt Rome itself. In 279 B.C. they were rampaging in Greece and Asia Minor. When the Roman armies started to move northwards, the nations they conquered in northern Italy, France, the Netherlands and Britain were mostly Celts. The modern languages of Welsh, Erse and Gaelic are Celtic.

The Germanic tribes were another group of people on the move. They first started to move into the Roman empire towards the end of the second century A.D. Mass migrations of these tribes began about two hundred years later when these peoples entered the Roman empire for protection from the attacks of the Huns—fierce warriors from Asia.

The Visigoths are an example of how some of these Germanic tribes came into the Roman empire for protection and then became attackers. Pursued by the Huns, the Visigoths moved west until they came to the river Danube, a boundary of the Roman empire. Here they asked the Romans for

Above: A Barbarian brooch set with stones from the seventh century.

Top: A detail from the relief on Trajan's column. The Roman soldiers are defending their position against the Dacians.

Left: The head of an Ostrogothic king of the 6th century.

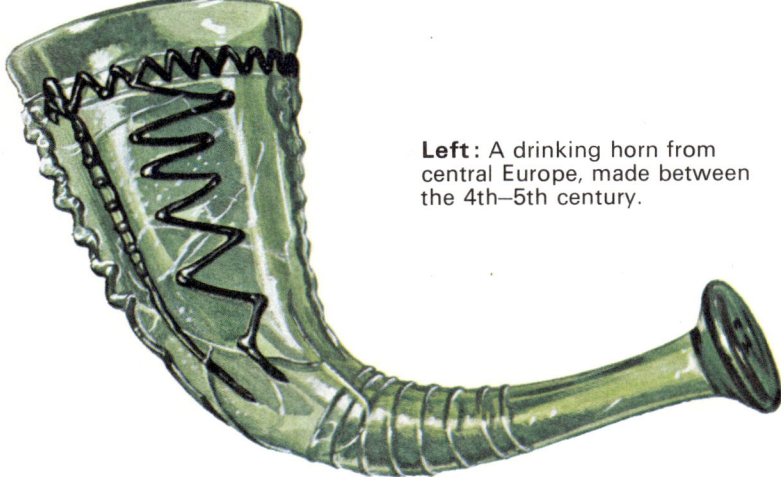

Left: A drinking horn from central Europe, made between the 4th–5th century.

permission to cross into safety. Many thousands of Visigoths entered the empire, but Roman officials cheated them of food and further angered them by not allowing the rest of their tribesmen to follow them. The Visigoths rebelled and defeated the Romans at Adrianople in A.D. 378. Later a Visigoth leader, Alaric, led his people west until they reached Rome itself. His troops sacked Rome in 410. Then they moved on through Europe and finally settled in southern Gaul and Spain.

Other Germanic groups such as the Vandals, Goths, Franks, Burgundians and Lombards now pushed into the empire. Their chieftains admired Rome and tried to imitate the Romans, and they became the new rulers of the Roman cities and provinces.

The Vandals crossed the river Rhine into Gaul and spread nto Spain. When they reached the southern tip of Spain they crossed into north Africa. Then they moved along the coast to Carthage where they built a fleet and attacked Rome from the south in 455.

In 476, the last Roman emperor, Romulus Augustulus, was forced to abdicate and the Roman empire of the west came to an end. Constantinople remained the capital of the Eastern Roman empire which continued for another thousand years.

The Angles, Saxons and Jutes sailed across the North Sea and attacked Britain. Britain had been abandoned by the Roman legions about the year 410, and the Anglo-Saxon attacks continued for several centuries. Eventually, they gained control over the native Britons, and called the country 'Angle-land' or 'England'.

Behind all these great movements of nations in the West lay trouble in central Asia. The Germanic tribes who came over the frontiers of the Roman empire were being attacked from behind by other nations from farther east. And behind them, like shepherds driving their sheep in front of them, came the terrible Huns.

The Huns were a nomadic nation of the plains of central Asia. They were short and ugly. They had tiny black eyes in shapeless

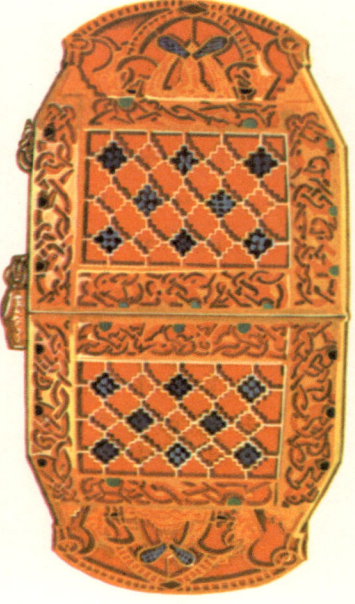

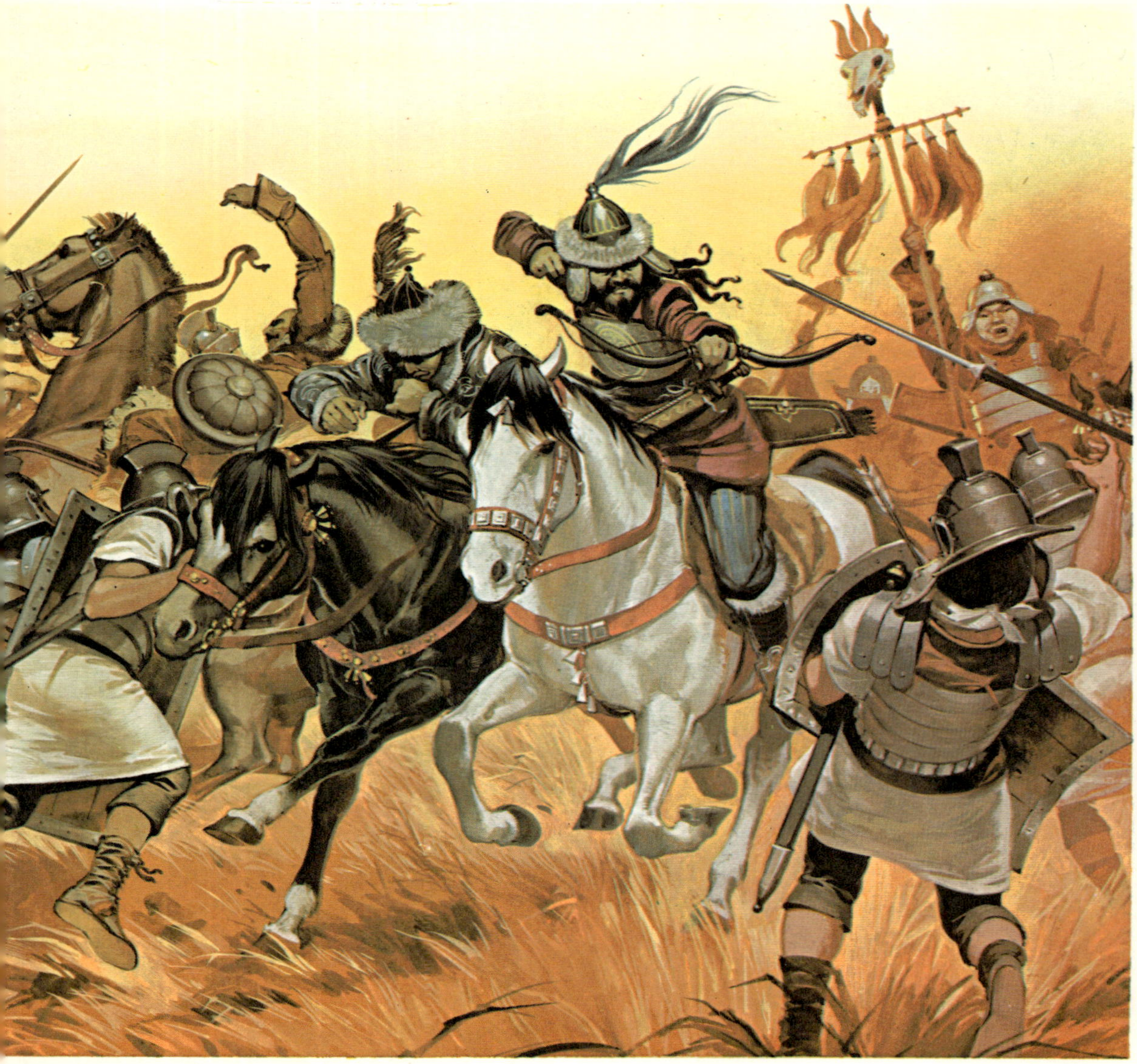

Left: The Huns attacked by dividing their forces and attacking an enemy army from all sides.

Below: An Anglo-Saxon shoulder brooch of the 7th century decorated in enamel, from the Sutton Hoo ship burial.

faces. They were bandy-legged, through riding on horseback almost from the time they were babies. They were great horsemen, used to riding for hundreds of miles. They were also expert archers.

In their own country the Huns had worked out a method for hunting wild animals. They would divide into several groups and encircle an area of countryside perhaps several hundreds of kilometres across. Gradually they would close in, until all the animals in the middle were trapped from all sides. They developed a signalling system to do this, which helped them to keep in touch with each other over hundreds of square kilometres.

When they went to war, they used the same system. An army trying to stop an army of Huns attacking them from the front, for instance, would suddenly find, to their surprise, another army of Huns coming up from behind. And then perhaps others closing in from either side. No wonder they took to their heels and ran. Then the Huns chased after them and killed as many as they could catch. Watching the advance of a Hunnish army was a terrifying sight. At night their campfires could be seen twinkling as far as the horizon in every direction. And behind them were only the smoking ruins of towns and villages. Long ago, a scribe of Sumeria, who had seen a similar army on the move, wrote on a clay tablet that they were like 'a host whose onslaught was like a hurricane, a people who had never known a city'.

For several years in the fifth century, the Huns made a vast camp on the plains of Hungary. Their leader was named Attila. Then, in the year A.D. 451, the whole army moved into Gaul, which is now France. There it was met and defeated, in one of the great battles of history, at Châlons-sur-Marne. In this battle the Romans, Goths and many other nations fought side by side against the Huns.

Not long afterwards Attila died. The Huns returned to central Asia. Later they climbed the mountain passes and swooped into India, where they destroyed the empire of Chandragupta II (see page 41).

On several later occasions other nations related to the Huns poured into eastern Europe. They included the Magyars, who founded Hungary, and the Turks. Meanwhile, the people of Europe had to deal with an equally fierce attack from another quarter. In the eighth century A.D. (that is, between the years 700 and 800) shiploads of pirates began to attack the coasts of eastern Europe. They came from Norway, Sweden and Denmark and were known as the Norsemen, or Vikings.

After a time, these raiders banded together to form a great army. They were fierce, savage robbers, looking for gold and slaves. They were also clever and energetic. They overran most of the western countries and even sailed into the Mediterranean and formed kingdoms in southern Italy and Sicily. In the north they crossed the ocean to Iceland and Greenland and even discovered America, which they called Vin-

land. In England they were at last beaten by the English king, Alfred the Great, in a decisive battle in 878. Then they began to settle and before long they adopted the Christian religion.

So Europe began to recover from the barbarian invasions. The barbarians had become civilized and had started to form new nations, from which the modern nations of Europe have grown.

The East, however, had to endure more invasions from central Asia. As we have already seen, the greatest of these was the invasion of the Mongols, in the thirteenth century. After doing tremendous damage, the Mongols settled and became civilized. On page 46 we read about the emperor Kublai Khan in his wonderful capital in China. And we read of how the Mongols crossed the Himalayan passes and founded a great empire in India. Mesopotamia, however, suffered most. There the Mongols destroyed the irrigation system around the rivers Tigris and Euphrates so thoroughly that it never really recovered, and now it is a barren land unable to support much agriculture.

Below: The Oseberg ship (9th century). A queen was buried with the ship she used for sailing in fine weather. The prow and gunwhale are beautifully carved and contained tents, beds, a wagon and sledges. The Oseberg ship was complete with all its gear; anchor, masts, gangway and oars. It was used for pleasure, unlike other ocean-going Viking ships.

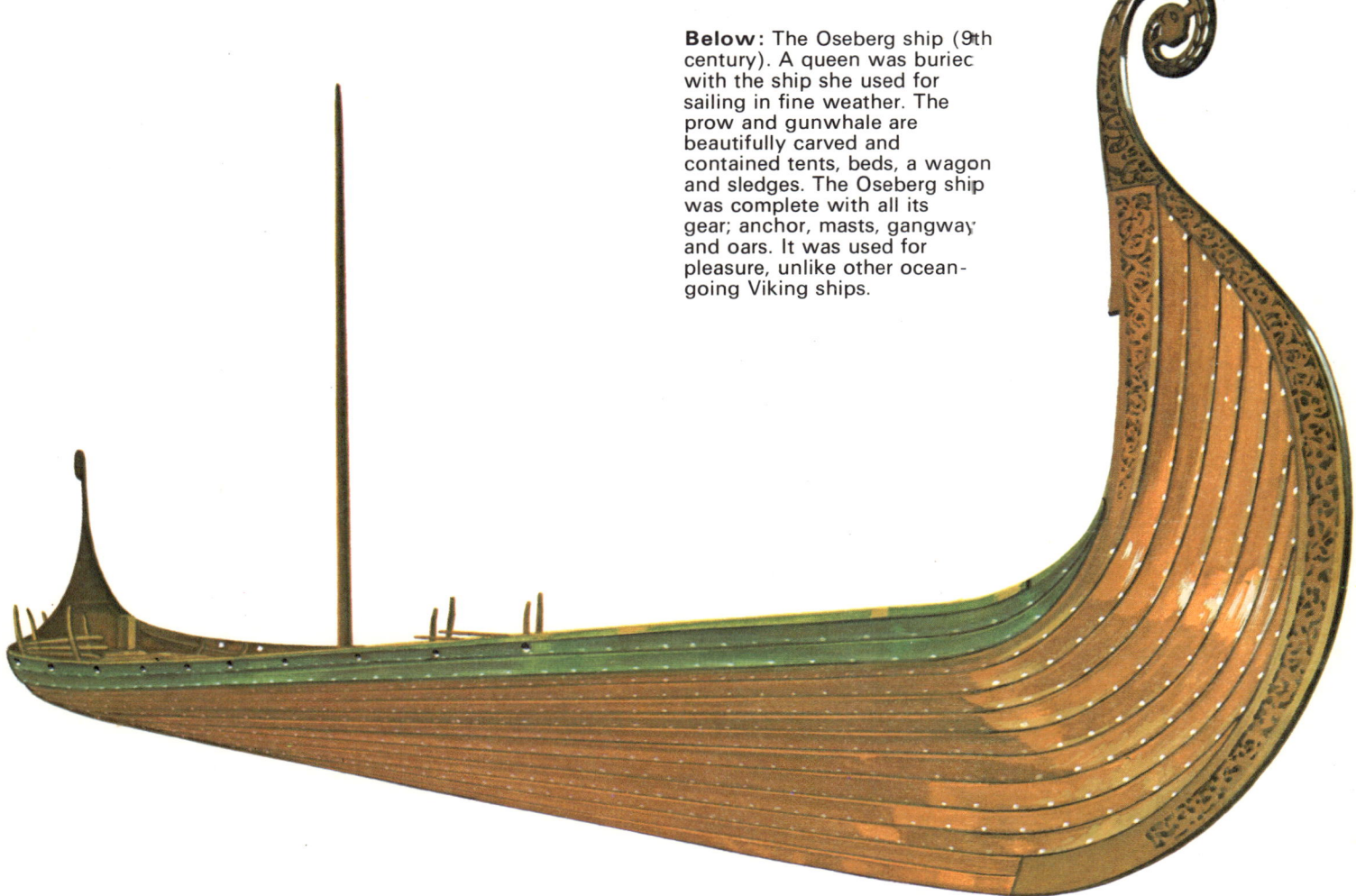

South & Central America

If we look at the map of South America we shall see a range of very high mountains all down the left or west side. They are called the Andes. They are some of the highest mountains on earth. The highest peaks are more than 6,000 metres high and are always covered with snow. The Andes are also a very long range of mountains. From north to south they reach for more than 7,200 kilometres. And for all that long distance they are very near the sea. Therefore, they are very steep mountains. Climbing from the sea coast to the summits of the mountains is like going upstairs. The paths are stony and steep. They cling to the sides of terrifying precipices. Sometimes they cross great chasms by means of fragile bridges. Swift rivers flow deep through these dark and terrifying chasms.

The central part of the Andes is now the country of Peru. Five hundred years ago Peru was much larger than it is now. It extended from near Quito (see map) to Santiago in Chile. That is about 5,232 kilometres. It was ruled by the Incas and was known as the empire of the Incas.

The Incas were similar people to the Indians of North America. Their skins were reddish brown. Many of their descendants live in Peru today. Many other tribes lived in the valleys of the Andes, but the Incas became the chief ones. They made war on most of the other tribes and dominated them for about fifty years.

They called themselves 'The Children of the Sun'. The sun was their god. They made golden images of the sun and hung them in their temples. When they conquered another tribe they made those people worship the sun, too.

Above: The Incas farmed by building terraced fields up the mountain sides. These fields prevented the soil being swept away and increased the amount of land available for farming.

Left: Map to show central America and part of South America. Notice the Andes mountains running down the side of South America.

Above: The Incas were amongst the finest stonemasons the world has ever seen. This building is still being used in Cuzco.

Left: The ruins of Machu Picchu, the lost city of the Inca. There are more than 100 stairways in these ruins which were re-discovered in 1912.

The head of the Incas was the emperor. He was known as *The* Inca. He was thought to be the representative of the Sun God on earth. So he, too, was worshipped. He was a very special person indeed. He sat on a golden throne and was dressed in clothes made of the finest wool. Anyone who came to see him had to walk barefoot.

The whole world was supposed to belong to him. Nobody else owned anything. Ordinary people were allowed to use land and shops, but they had to pay rent or taxes to the Inca for these things. The Inca was like the father of a great family. Everybody in the family had a job to do. If he did it properly, he had a right to food, clothes, a house and anything else he needed. If he was lazy, he was punished. Children and people too old to work, or who were ill, were looked after well.

The Inca lived in a palace in the mountain city of Cuzco. Near the palace was the magnificent Temple of the Sun. Palaces and temples and other important buildings were built of stone. The Incas were great builders. They could fit together huge blocks of stone so well that no mortar was needed to fasten them. They dug gold and silver from mines in the mountains and made wonderful and beautiful ornaments from them. Because of its colour, gold was sacred to the Sun.

Ordinary people lived in huts built of dried clay. They grew crops on terraces in the mountain valleys. Many of the fields were irrigated by streams of water. The farmers grew maize instead of wheat. They also grew potatoes, tomatoes, cocoa, pineapples and many other crops. These crops were unknown in Europe before Europeans discovered America. They used llamas as farm animals. They had no horses, cattle or sheep. The wool they used for their clothes came from the llamas, especially from a special sort of llama called the alpaca. The children kept guinea-pigs as pets. Guinea-pigs, as well as the other crops mentioned, originated in South America.

Below: A silver alpaca Llama. An Inca figurine made between 1450–1540.

Left: Quipu knots. This complicated system of knots was used for keeping records.

Below: A pottery figure showing a labourer going out into the fields.

Llamas carried burdens on their backs but did not pull carts or farm implements. They were not strong enough to carry a man. The farmers cultivated the land by digging it, with a special sort of spade. Each spring the land around a village was divided out among the village people. Some fields were for the Inca and others for the priests in the Temple. Work had to be done on these fields first. The other fields were for the ordinary people. Life was quite hard, but no-one went hungry. Also there were many festivals at which people feasted and danced and enjoyed themselves.

The Incas managed their empire without two things which we would think essential. They had no system of writing. And they never learned how to make a wheel.

The Incas relied on a complicated system of knots, tied in short lengths of string for keeping records. These knots were known as *quipus*. Some quipus still survive, but no-one is really sure how to read them.

Everything had to be carried on the backs of either men or llamas because there were no wheels. The Incas made a wonderful system of roads to hold together their immense empire and trained runners carried messages and goods. The runners worked by relays. Each runner would run as fast as he could for a few miles and then hand over his load to the next man, who would be waiting for him. By this system, messages could travel as much as 400 kilometres a day. And the Inca in his palace at Cuzco would have for supper fish caught fresh from the sea that morning, more than 200 kilometres away.

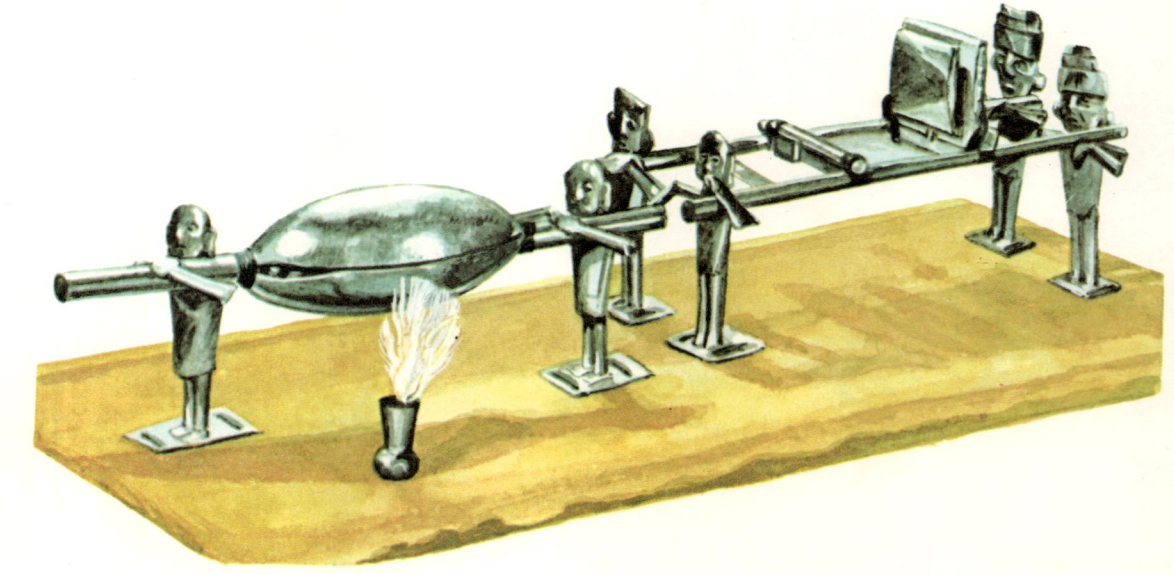

Right: A funeral procession of small figures in silver from an Inca grave in Peru. The litter took the body, and the container probably carried belongings which were interred in the grave.

Left: A gold figure of an Inca water carrier.

Below: A painted wooden beaker or *keru*, depicting a scene from a ceremonial procession.

Post-houses stood at intervals of about 20 kilometres along the roads. Here travellers could rest and eat. Supplies of food were always kept there. Often the roads had to cross great ravines. Bridges were made of strong ropes, cleverly woven. They swayed in the wind but were very safe.

The Inca Empire did not last long. Inca armies began conquering their neighbours about the year A.D. 1440, fifty years before Christopher Columbus sailed to America. By 1532 their Empire was complete. A civil war had just been fought, and the winner, the Inca Atahualpa, was resting after the battles. As he was preparing to return in triumph to his capital, a little Spanish army arrived on the coast of Peru. Their leader was named Pizarro.

Atahualpa was curious to see these white men, so he had them brought to his capital. There they kidnapped him, held him to ransom and finally killed him. Within a few months Pizarro had overthrown the mighty Empire of the Incas.

In the centuries which followed, Spaniards and Indians intermarried. The present people of Peru and the neighbouring countries are of mixed Spanish and Indian blood. And nearly half of them still speak Quechua, the old Inca language.

While the Inca Empire was growing in South America, another equally magnificent one was being established in Central America. This was the Empire of the Aztecs. Their capital city, Tenochtitlan, was where Mexico City now stands.

Far Left: This wooden face mask was used as an Inca tomb offering. Originally it had human hair.

Left: A pottery jar; the neck is in the form of a human head and the body is decorated with animal symbols.

The city was built on islands in the middle of a great lake. The only way to reach it was across huge stone causeways. The largest causeway was nearly five kilometres long. At intervals there were gaps in the causeways. They were spanned by wooden bridges which could be taken away if an enemy threatened to attack.

In the year A.D. 1519, when Europeans first saw Tenochtitlan, the city held as many people in it as the largest cities of Europe. It had become so crowded that many people were living on boats on the lake. The peasants had learned how to make floating gardens. They were made of earth, held together by wickerwork and floating on great logs. Gardeners grew vegetables and fruit on them.

The empire of the Aztecs extended for many, many kilometres around the city. Like the Incas, the Aztecs were conquerors. At one time, they were just one tribe among many who lived in Mexico. They became great warriors and made most of the other tribes their subjects.

The Aztecs and the other tribes of Central America were reddish-brown in colour. The Aztec nobles wore splendid clothes and magnificent feathered head-dresses and cloaks. Warriors and priests often wore the skins of animals, with the heads attached as masks. Ordinary people's clothes, which included ponchos, were made of wool and vegetable fibre.

The Aztecs did not understand the use of the wheel. Nor did they know about iron. Their weapons and tools were of a specially sharp black stone, known as obsidian. They mounted blades of obsidian into carved handles of wood. But the Aztecs had one thing that the Incas lacked. They had learned how to write. They kept records, in a form of picture writing, in books made of parchment.

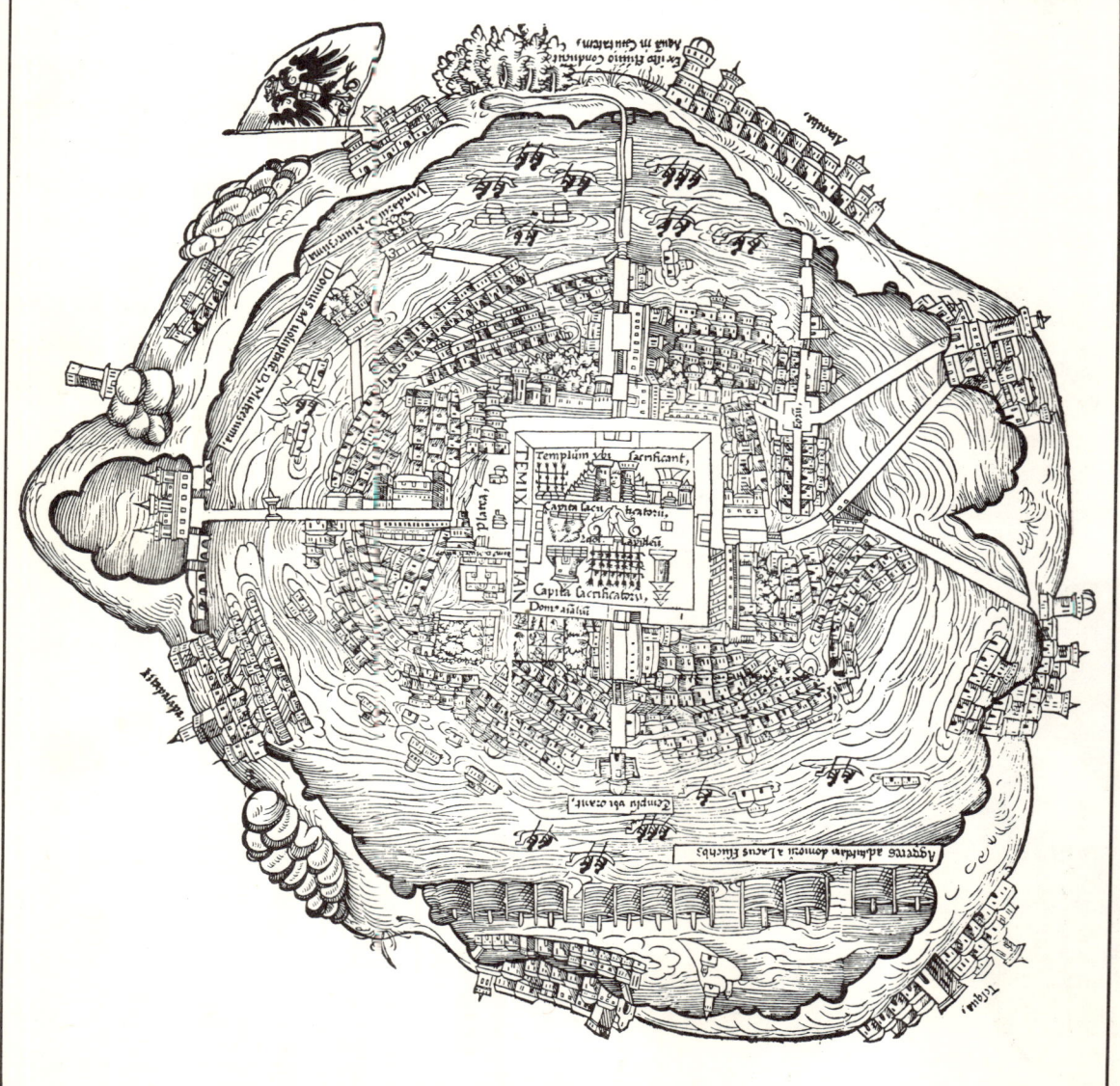

Left: A plan of the city of Tenochtitlan made by Cortés. This great city was approached by causeways across Lake Texcoco.

Below: An Aztec mask, one of the many gifts sent by Moctezuma to Cortés. The Aztec ruler believed Cortés to be the god Quetzalcoatl.

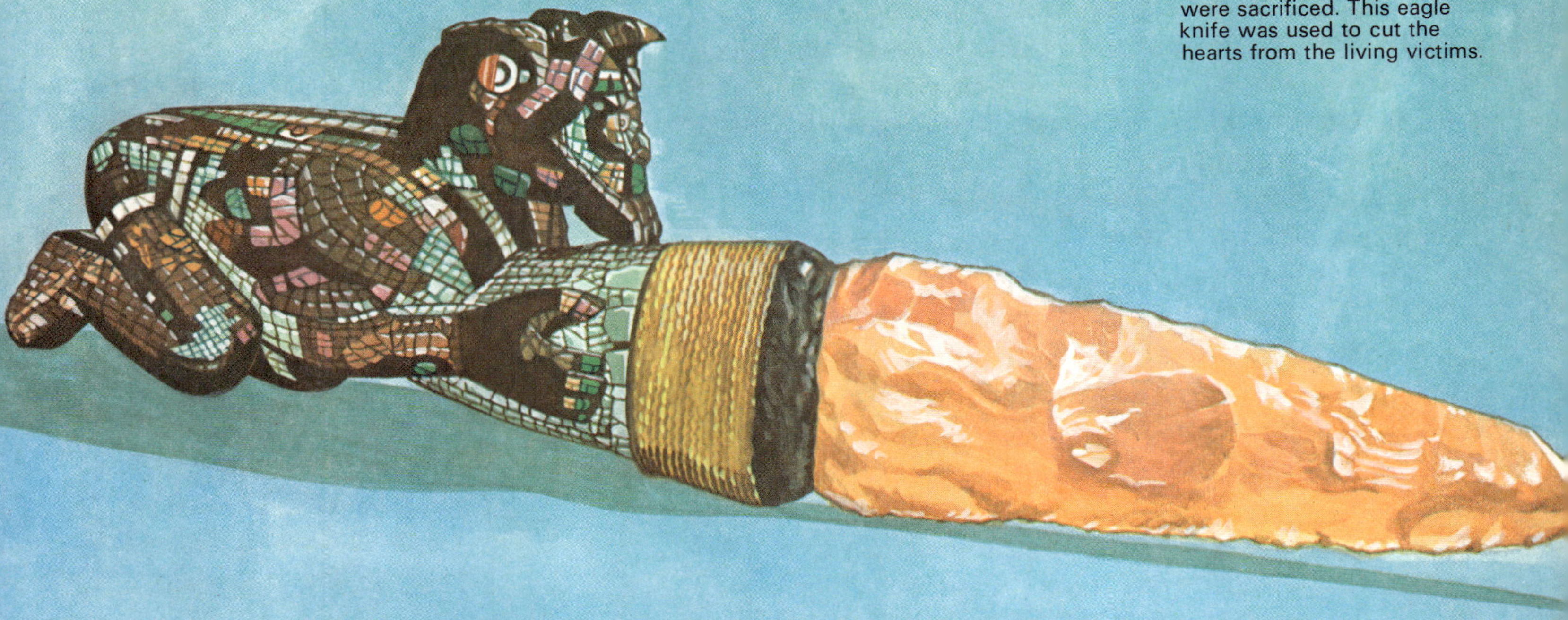

The Aztecs believed that the Sun needed blood to keep it on its course, and it was their duty to provide nourishment by perpetual human sacrifice. They made sacred wars on their neighbours, and the prisoners were sacrificed. This eagle knife was used to cut the hearts from the living victims.

The Aztecs were hated by most of their neighbours. This was because they had a very bloodthirsty religion. They worshipped gods whom they thought had to be kept satisfied with human sacrifices. In the heart of their great city stood high pyramids, with steps to the top. On the very summit were altars, where victims were sacrificed. The victim was laid on his back on an altar, his chest cut open with a sharp knife and his heart torn out. It was thought that their god fed on human hearts.

These sacrifices went on ceaselessly. The purpose of the wars that the Aztecs were always making on their neighbours was to capture prisoners for sacrifice. In one war as many as 20,000 prisoners were captured and sacrificed.

The Aztecs had another god, whose name was Quetzalcoatl. He had once visited them, hundreds of years ago, and had taught them many things. He promised to return one day. In pictures he was shown as a white man with a beard.

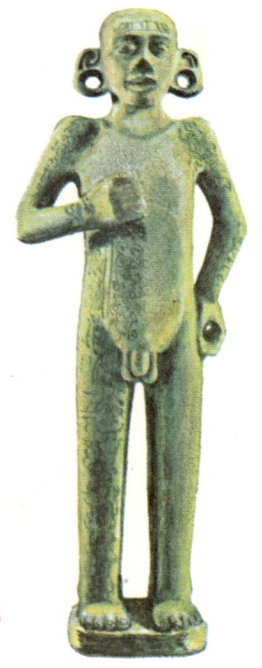

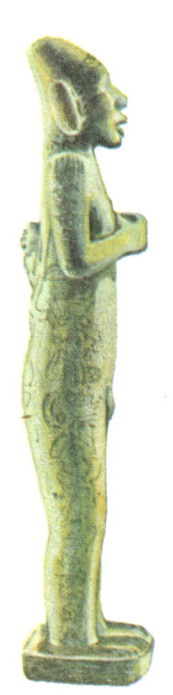

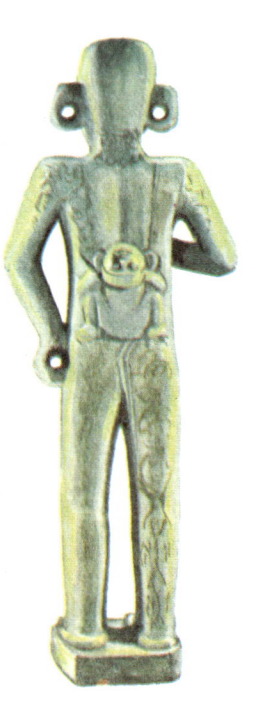

Left: The god Quetzalcoatl as a young man. The Aztecs thought that Cortés was Quetzalcoatl and greeted him with gifts.

In the year 1519, nearly thirty years after Columbus had discovered America, a Spaniard named Cortes landed with a small army on the coast of Mexico. He was a white man with a beard. The Aztecs wondered whether he might be their god returned as he said he would. So they hestitated until it was too late. Cortés made friends with many of the neighbouring tribes, who hated the Aztecs. Then he made war on the Aztecs, conquered them and destroyed much of their wonderful city.

Mexico became a Spanish colony. The Spaniards intermarried with the Aztecs and other tribes, and nowadays most Mexicans have mixed blood.

Long before the Aztecs created their empire there was another great civilization in Central America. It was the civilization of the Mayas. They had two empires, one after the other. The first was in what are now the republics of Guatemala and Honduras. This began in the fourth century A.D., and lasted until about A.D. 800. The second was in Yucatán (in southern Mexico) and lasted from 800 to about A.D. 1350. The Mayas migrated, for some unknown reason, from the first area to the second in Yucatán.

Most of the Mayas lived in villages and cultivated small fields, where they grew maize, pumpkins and other crops. But they had very powerful priests, who persuaded them to build great temples.

These temples were in the form of pyramids. The priests said that a new pyramid must be built every fifty-two years. Often this was done by building a new one around an older one. When archaeologists excavate one of these pyramids they find it is like peeling an onion. There is a whole series of pyramids, one inside another.

The period of fifty-two years was decided on after studying the calendar. The Mayas ruled their lives by the calendar. For generations Maya priests studied the stars until they were able to work out a very accurate calendar indeed. It was quite as accurate as the one we use today. The priests could calculate the length of a day to a fraction of a second. They knew the

Above: The temple of the warriors at Chichen Itza encloses the shrine of Chac, the Mayan rain-cloud spirit.

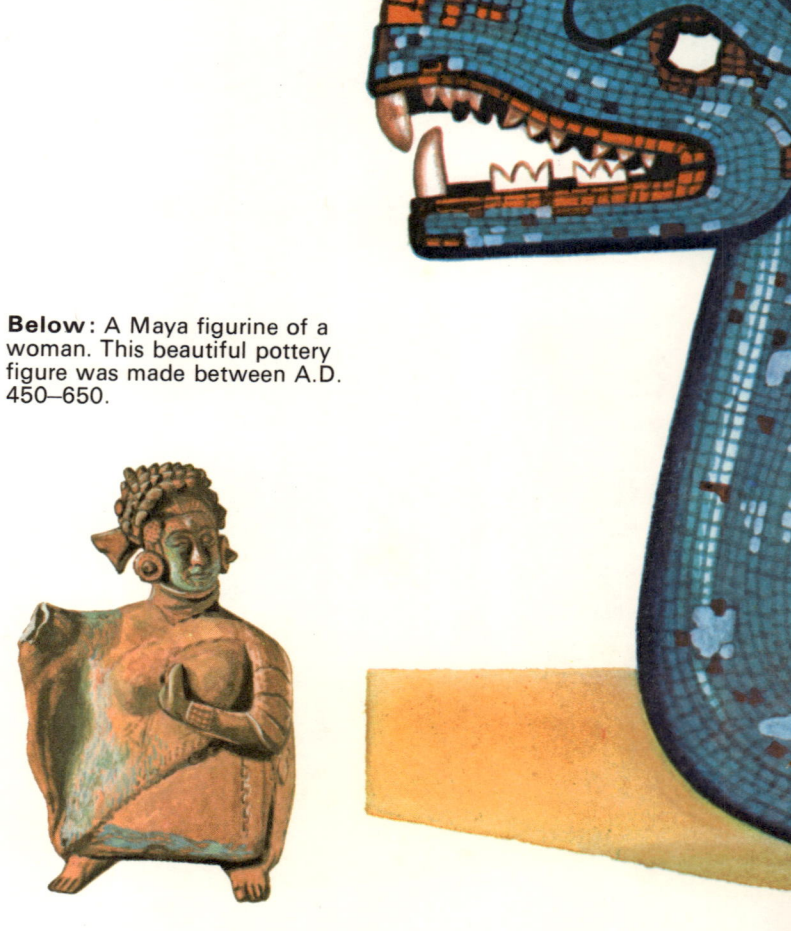

Below: A Maya figurine of a woman. This beautiful pottery figure was made between A.D. 450–650.

distance of the moon from the earth. They also studied the movements of the planets, including Venus.

The jungles of Central America are studded with the ruins of pyramid temples. Some of them are now covered in earth and overgrown with trees, so that they look like hills. Some have been excavated, but many more have not. There are deep wells near some of the temples. People who used to come to the temples to worship threw gifts into the wells, much as we throw pennies into wishing wells. In recent years divers have recovered many treasures of gold, copper, jade and other precious stones from these wells. We have been able to learn a great deal about the Mayas and the things they were able to do from these wells.

No-one knows why the ancient Maya cities fell into ruins. Perhaps the people rebelled against the rule of the priests. While all the magnificent temples were being built, the people still lived in mud and timber houses.

Maya people still do. There are about two million of them, who speak the Maya language. They live in villages in many parts of Central America, gaining their living mostly by farming and fishing.

One of the curious things about these American empires is that they had so little contact with each other. The Mayan empires flourished and died before the Aztec empire was formed. Both the Aztec and Inca empires were at the height of their power when Europeans first discovered America, but, as far as we know, they had never even heard of each other.

Below: An Aztec serpent. This beautiful turquoise mosaic was probably worn as an ornament on the chest.

Index

Figures in bold refer to illustrations